MASTERING OHIO'S FOURTH GRADE PROFICIENCY TESTS IN READING AND WRITING

JAMES KILLORAN

STUART ZIMMER

MARK JARRETT

JARRETT PUBLISHING COMPANY

East Coast Office
P.O. Box 1460
Ronkonkoma, NY 11779
631-981-4248

West Coast Office
10 Folin Lane
Lafayette, CA 94549
925-906-9742

1-800-859-7679   Fax: 631-588-4722
www.jarrettpub.com

This book includes material from many different sources. Occasionally it is not possible to determine if a particular source is copyrighted, and if so, who is the copyright owner. Every effort has been made to trace the ownership of all copyrighted material and to secure the necessary permissions to reprint these selections. If there has been a copyright infringement with any material in this book, it is unintentional. We extend our sincerest apologies and would be happy to make immediate and appropriate restitution upon proof of copyright ownership.

Grateful acknowledgment is made to the following publishers to reprint the copyrighted materials listed below:

Black Dog and Leventhal Publishers for "Alvin Ailey" by Andrea Davis Pinkney in *African American Read Aloud Stories*. ©1998.

Carolrhoda Books for the story "How Horses Communicate" by Dorothy H. Patent in *Cricket Magazine,* © August, 1998.

Follett Press for the poem, "City, City" by Marci Ridlon in *That Was Summer,* © 1969.

Greenwillow Books for the story "The Wolf and the Dog" in *The Acorn Tree and Other Folktales,* © 1995.

Random House for the poems, "Sea Calm" and "We're All In The Phone Book" by Langston Hughes appearing in *The Collected Poems of Langston Hughes,* edited by Arnold Rampersaud © 1995.

Simon and Schuster for the stories "The Shoemaker and the Elves" and "How Big Mouth Wrestled the Giant" in *Diane Goode's Book of Giants and Little People,* © 1997. For "The Devoted Son and the Thief," "The Emperor and the Peasant Boy," in *The Book of Virtues For Young People,* edited by William J. Bennett, © 1997. For "Earth and Water and Sky" by Bryan A. Bushemi, and "Danger From the Sky" by Barbara Saffer, in *Cricket Magazine,* © October, 1998.

Scholastic Inc. for the article, *Wolves* by Seymour Simon, © 1993.

Copyright 2000 by Jarrett Publishing Company

All rights reserved. No part of this book may be reproduced in any form or by any means, including electronic, photographic, mechanical, or by any device for storage and retrieval of information, without the express written permission of the publisher. Requests for permission to make copies of any part of this book should be mailed to:

Jarrett Publishing Company
Post Office Box 1460
19 Cross Street
Ronkonkoma, New York 11779

ISBN 1-882422-52-X
Printed in the United States of America
by Malloy Lithographing, Inc., Ann Arbor, Michigan
First Edition
10 9 8 7 6 5 4 3 2 1   03 02 01 00

ACKNOWLEDGMENTS

The authors would like to thank the following teachers and supervisors who helped review the manuscript. Their collective comments, suggestions and recommendations have proved invaluable in preparing this book.

Cynthia Aulisio
A teacher at Denison Elementary School
Cleveland Municipal Schools

Kim Kozbial-Hess
A teacher at Fall-Meyer Elementary School
Toledo Public Schools

Melissa Krempasky
A teacher at North Linden Elementary School
Columbus Public Schools

Cover design, layout, graphics, and typesetting:
Burmar Technical Corporation, Albertson, N.Y.

This book is dedicated...

to my wife Donna and my children Christian, Carrie, and Jesse
— *James Killoran*

to my wife Joan, my children Todd and Ronald, and
my grandchildren Jared and Katie
— *Stuart Zimmer*

to my wife Gośka and my children Alexander and Julia
— *Mark Jarrett*

TABLE OF CONTENTS

INTRODUCTION

CHAPTER 1: USEFUL TOOLS FOR READING AND WRITING 3
  Applying Question Words 3
  Visualizing Information 4
    Topic or Subject Maps 5
    Sequence Maps 6
    Venn Diagrams 7
  Practice Exercises 9

UNIT 1: READING

Section 1: Types of Readings

CHAPTER 2: FICTION AND POETRY 15
  Stories 15
  Poetry 20
  Practice Exercises 22

CHAPTER 3: NONFICTION 27
  The Topic Sentence 27
  Supporting Details 27
  Finding the Main Idea 29
  Practice Exercises 30

Section 2: Types of Questions

CHAPTER 4: ANSWERING MULTIPLE-CHOICE QUESTIONS 33
  Topic Questions 34
  Comprehension Questions 35
    Detail Questions 35
    Sequence Questions 37
    Explanation Questions 39
    Compare-and-Contrast Questions 41
    Vocabulary Questions 42
  Inferential Questions 44
    Drawing-Conclusion Questions 44
    Prediction Questions 45
    Library Resource Questions 47
    Theme Questions 49

    Test-taking Strategies 50
        Step 1: Identify the Type of Reading 50
        Step 2: Read with a Purpose 51
        Step 3: Answer the Questions 52

CHAPTER 5: ANSWERING OPEN-ENDED QUESTIONS 53
    Questions that Focus on Overall Meaning 54
        Summarizing a Story 54
        Retelling a Story 55
    Questions that Focus on Specific Details 56
        What Questions 57
        How Questions 59
        Why Questions 61
    Completing Graphic Organizers 62
        The Venn Diagram 62
        A Two-Column Chart 63
        The Wheel Graphic 64
    Practice Exercises 65

CHAPTER 6: CHECKING YOUR UNDERSTANDING 69

UNIT 2: WRITING

CHAPTER 7: THE ELEMENTS OF GOOD WRITING 83
    The Characteristics of Good Writing 85
        A Clear Focus 85
        A Logical Organization 86
        Clear and Expressive Language 87
        Use of Writing Conventions 88
    Organizing Your Written Response 89
        Introduction 89
        Body 89
        Conclusion 89
    The Writing Process 90
        Step 1: Analyze the Question 90
        Step 2: Plan and Pre-Write 90
        Step 3: Write Your Answer 91
        Step 4: Revise and Edit 91
    Practice Exercises 93

CHAPTER 8: WRITING A FICTIONAL NARRATIVE 95
Writing a Fictional Narrative 95
   Setting 96
   Characters 97
   Plot 97
   Conclusion 99
Practice Exercises 100

CHAPTER 9: WRITING ABOUT YOUR PERSONAL EXPERIENCES 105
How to Write about Your Personal Experiences 105
   Pre-Writing 105
   A Narrative about Your Personal Experiences 107
   Introduction to Your Essay 109
   The Body of Your Essay 109
   Conclusion to Your Essay 111
Practice Exercises 112

CHAPTER 10: WRITING A REPORT 117
How to Write a Report 118
   Pre-Writing Section 120
   Writing Your Report 123
A Model Report 124
Practice Exercises 125

CHAPTER 11: WRITING LETTERS, JOURNALS, AND DIRECTIONS 131
Writing Letters 131
   Practice Writing a Letter 132
Writing a Letter to the Editor 133
   Helpful Hints 133
   A Model Letter to the Editor 134
   Practice Writing a Letter to the Editor 134
Writing a Thank-You Letter 136
   Helpful Hints 136
   Practice Writing a Thank-You Letter 136

    Writing an Invitation 138
        Helpful Hints 138
        Practice Writing An Invitation 138
    Keeping a Journal 140
        Helpful Hints 140
        A Model Journal 140
        Practice Writing Journal Entries 140
    Giving Directions 142
        Helpful Hints 142
        A Model Set of Directions 143
        Practice Giving Written Directions 143
    Practice Exercises 145

CHAPTER 12: CHECKING YOUR UNDERSTANDING 147
    Exercise A: A Fictional Narrative Essay 150
    Exercise B: A Letter of Invitation 153

UNIT 3: FINAL PRACTICE TESTS IN READING AND WRITING

A PRACTICE TEST IN READING 156
    Directions for the Reading Section of the Practice Test 157
    Fictional Story: "How Big Mouth Wrestled the Giant" 158
    Poem by Langston Hughes 162
    Biography: Alvin Ailey 165
    Almanac Article: Dinosaurs 169

A PRACTICE TEST IN WRITING 172
    Directions for the Writing Section of the Practice Test 173
    Exercise A: A Fictional Narrative 179
    Exercise B: A Friendly Letter 182

APPENDICES

A HANDBOOK OF GRAMMAR AND WRITING MECHANICS 185
INTERPRETING DIFFERENT TYPES OF DATA 201

NOTES

INTRODUCTION

This introductory chapter takes a look at some useful tools that will help you to prepare for Ohio's Fourth Grade Proficiency Tests in Reading and Writing. These tools include using "question" words to guide your thinking when you read or listen to any story or reading passage. They also include techniques for recalling important information.

CHAPTER 1

USEFUL TOOLS FOR READING AND WRITING

APPLYING QUESTION WORDS

In reading any story or informational passage, you should think of yourself as a reporter. When a reporter is assigned to cover a new story, he or she must gather information. To get the total picture, reporters ask certain basic questions to help focus their thinking. These are the **question words** they ask:

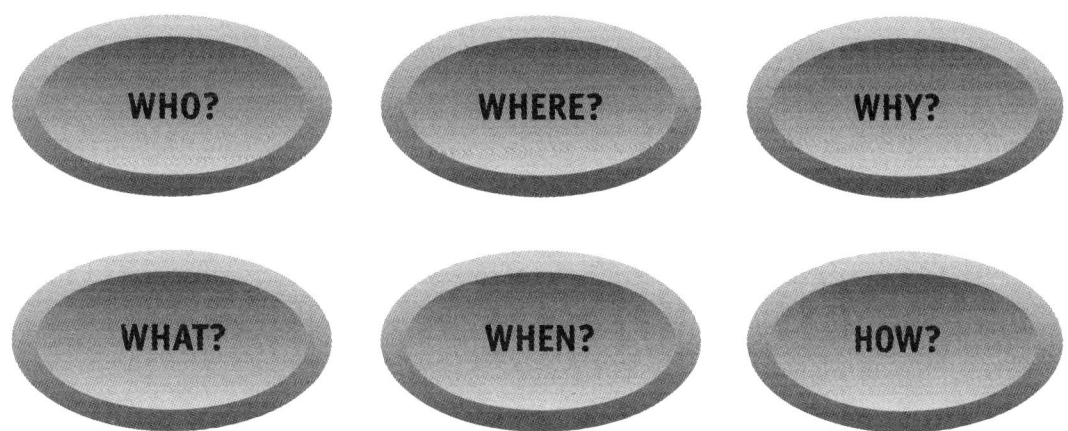

Let's take a closer look at each of these question words to see how they act as guides when you examine new information.

3

★ **Who questions** ask you to *identify a person or character.*

★ **What questions** ask you about the *details of something.* They can refer to an object, activity, or event.

★ **When questions** ask you for the *time an event or activity happens* or has happened.

★ **Where questions** ask you for the *place in which an event happens* or has happened.

★ **Why questions** ask for the *reasons* something has taken place.

★ **How questions** ask you about *the way something happened.*

Whenever you read or listen to a story or reading selection, try to keep these **question words** in mind. They will help you get a better idea of what you have read or heard.

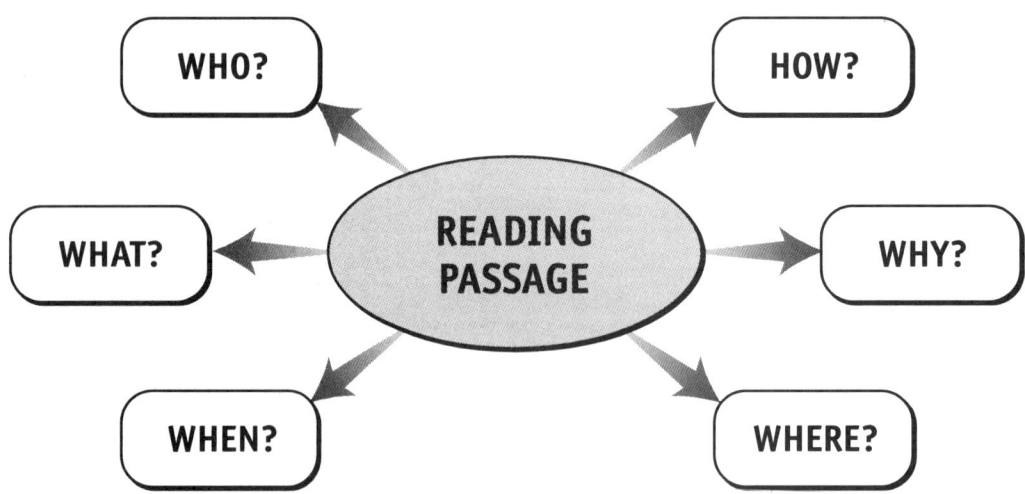

VISUALIZING INFORMATION

The **Fourth Grade Proficiency Tests in Reading and Writing** will require you to interpret different kinds of reading passages. To understand what you read, it often helps to visualize or "see" this information.

One way that people visualize information is to make a graphic organizer. A **graphic organizer** is a picture or diagram that turns words into a picture. The picture highlights important parts of the reading and shows how they are related. Let's look at three types of graphic organizers that can help you organize information you read.

TOPIC OR SUBJECT MAPS

You can create a *topic* or *subject map,* also called a "word cluster" or "web," by putting the main topic or idea of a reading in the center of the page. Then surround this topic or idea with supporting facts and details. Let's see how this is done by examining a reading about a boy named Alex.

MY FRIEND ALEX

Alex is my best friend at school. He is very smart, just like his mother. He is very friendly with his close friends, but is often shy when meeting strangers. He is tall for his age and is one of the best players on the school's basketball team.

PRACTICE COMPLETING A TOPIC MAP
Directions: Fill in the blank boxes with words that help to describe Alex.

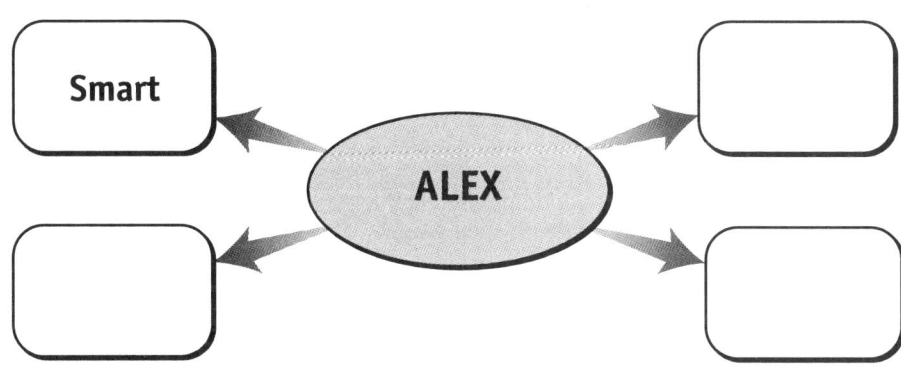

Notice how the graphic organizer is completed by finding the words that describe Alex. The reading selection told us he was "smart" and "tall." Ask yourself: *What other words in the reading help to describe Alex?*

This type of graphic organizer is best used when an idea, character, place or event is described. It can help you to see easily the details that make up that person, thing or idea.

SEQUENCE MAPS

Many reading passages describe a series of events. A *sequence map* can help you trace how these events developed over time. This type of map presents events in the order in which they occurred.

Let's see how to create a sequence map. First read the story about Julia's class trip to the zoo.

JULIA'S CLASS TRIP TO THE ZOO

Julia was excited when she awoke that morning. Her class was making its first school trip. Almost as soon as she arrived at school, her entire class boarded a yellow school bus. After a short drive, they arrived at the zoo. First, the class visited the monkeys and apes. Julia and her classmates couldn't help but laugh at the funny antics of the chimpanzees. Next, they saw the tigers and lions. After they saw the giraffes and elephants, it was already time to go home.

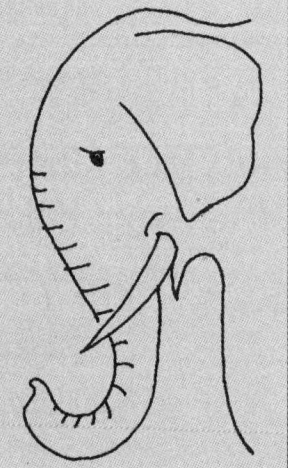

PRACTICE COMPLETING A SEQUENCE MAP
Directions: Fill in the boxes on the following page to show the sequence of events in the story. The first two boxes have been completed for you.

Julia wakes up in the morning very excited.

Julia arrives at school and gets into the bus.

You complete: _____

You complete: _____

You complete: _____

This type of graphic organizer is best used when you want to show how the events in a story go, in order, from one action to the next.

VENN DIAGRAMS

A **Venn diagram** is a useful way to visualize or show information when you wish to compare or contrast things. It uses overlapping ovals to show how two or more things are similar or different. Features that are the same for both are placed in the area where the ovals overlap. Features that are different are placed in the parts of the ovals that do not overlap.

PRACTICE COMPLETING A VENN DIAGRAM
Directions: Read the story below. Then complete the Venn diagram.

CHANTAL AND LIONEL

Lionel and Chantal are brother and sister. They grew up in the same house. When it came to eating, Lionel liked chicken and hamburgers, while Chantal liked fruit and vegetables. Both enjoyed ice cream for dessert. Lionel loved watching television, especially sports programs. Chantal, on the other hand, loved to write letters to her friends.

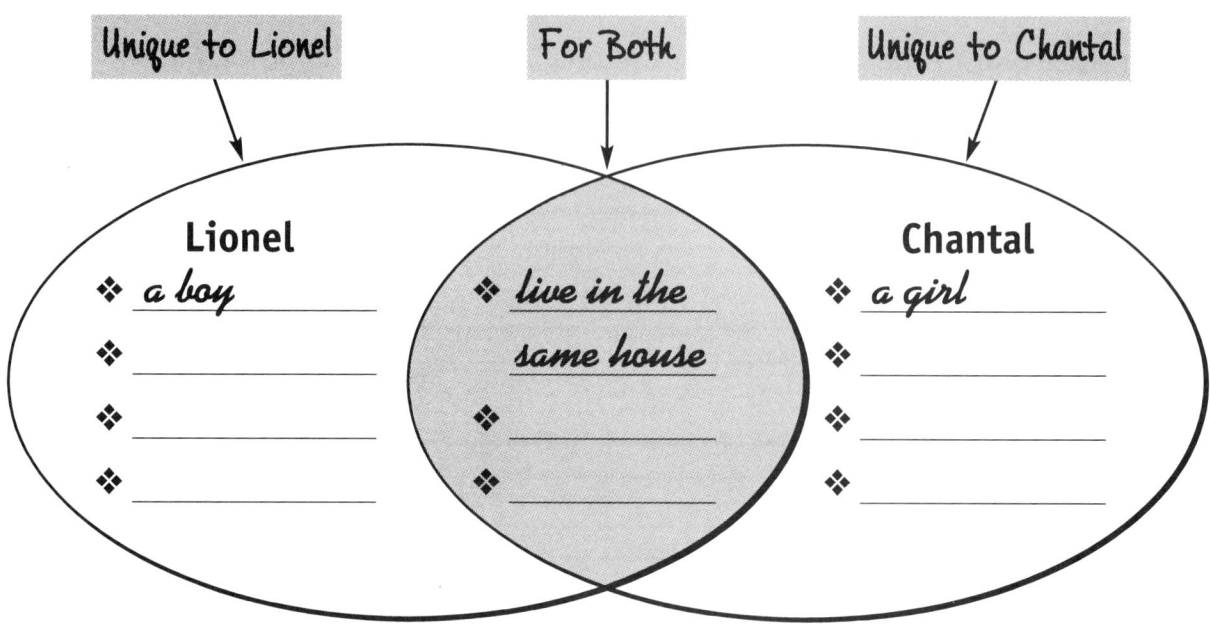

There are other ways to present a Venn diagram besides using ovals. You can also present the information using rectangles or circles:

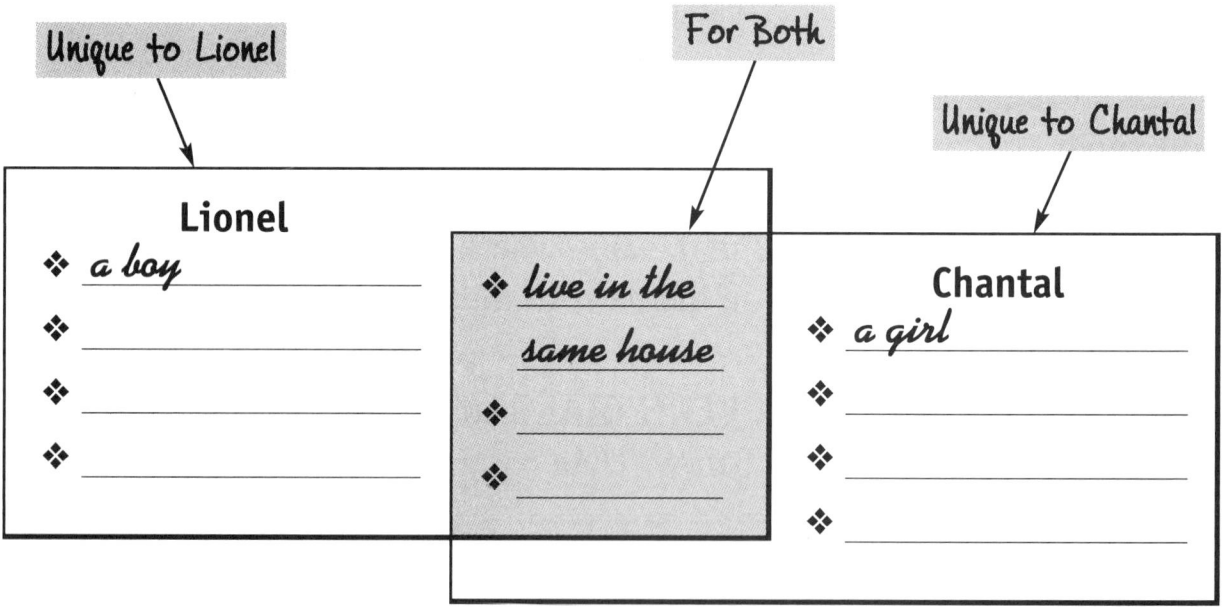

These three types of graphic organizers — **topic maps, sequence maps,** and **Venn diagrams** — can be used to organize almost any information you read. You can use these same organizers to jot down your ideas before you start to write a composition. We will refer to these ways of organizing information throughout the rest of the book. You will also learn about two more ways to diagram information in Chapter 5.

Practice Exercises

Directions: Read the passage below and then answer the questions that follow.

THE WOLF AND THE DOG

One day a starving wolf came out of the forest. Soon he met a big, strong, handsome dog. "Good morning," said the wolf to the dog, "You look very happy and well fed. Where have you found food this cold winter?"

The dog answered, "I am fortunate.[1] I don't have to find food. My master feeds me."

The wolf looked suspiciously at the dog. "Hmm," he said. "What do you do for your master?"

"Not much," answered the dog. "I go for walks with him and fetch sticks for him. During the evenings I sleep by his chair and am faithful to him. It's not a bad life. Last night I had roast beef, mashed potatoes, chicken and cheese for supper." The dog licked his chops, remembering his wonderful dinner.

"Don't tell me about such things!" cried the wolf. "It makes my stomach growl. How fortunate you are!"

---

[1] lucky

continued

"Why don't you come home with me?" said the dog. "You look a little like a dog. After a good meal, a bath and brushing, I'm sure my master would give you to his servant."

"Oh, how can I thank you?" said the wolf as they walked toward the master's house. Then the wolf noticed something around the dog's neck. "What are you wearing around your neck?" he asked.

"Oh," replied the dog, "that's nothing. It is only my collar."

"What is a collar?" asked the wolf. "Why do you wear it?"

"No reason," said the dog. "It is something my master uses to chain me up at night."

"Chain you up!" shouted the wolf in disbelief. "You mean you are tied up at night? I love to roam through the forest at night. If I come home with you, would I be chained up like you?"

"Of course," answered the dog. "Believe me, that is a very small price to pay for all the good things my master gives me. Hurry up, my friend. It is almost time for lunch."

But the wolf did not hear him, for he had run away. "Chained up all night," thought the wolf as he ran back to the forest. "I would rather go hungry and have my freedom than be fed and chained up like that!"

CHAPTER 1: USEFUL TOOLS FOR READING AND WRITING 11

A. List the events in the boxes to show the correct order or sequence of events in the story. The first two boxes of the sequence map have already been completed for you.

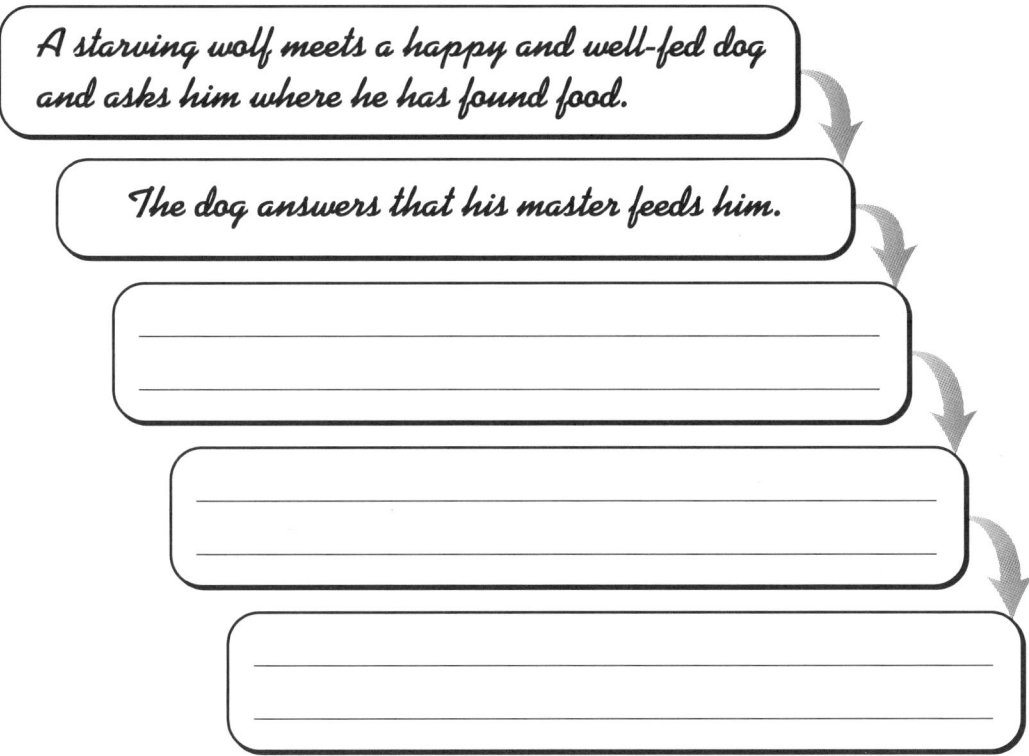

A starving wolf meets a happy and well-fed dog and asks him where he has found food.

The dog answers that his master feeds him.

B. Fill in this organizer by thinking of questions that would apply to the story. The first question has been completed for you.

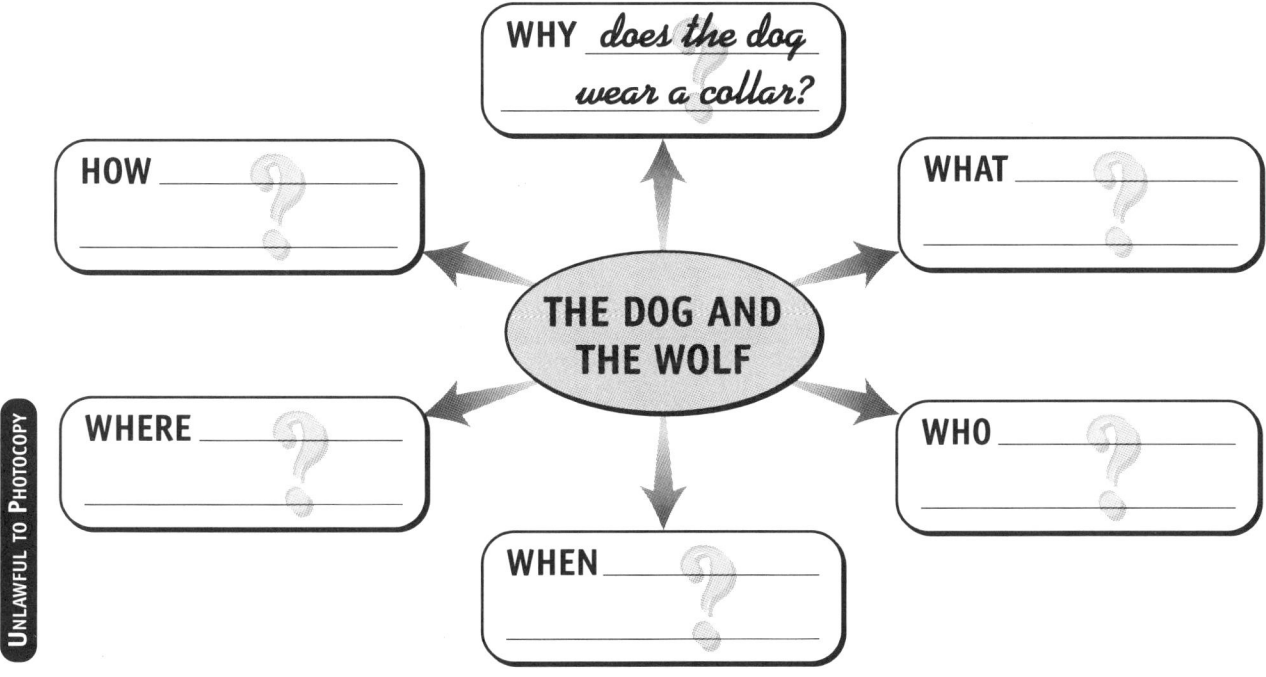

WHY *does the dog wear a collar?*

HOW

WHAT

WHERE

WHO

WHEN

THE DOG AND THE WOLF

Now answer each of the questions that you have written on page 11.

★ **Why:** *It is used to chain him up at night.*

★ **What:**

★ **Who:**

★ **When:**

★ **Where:**

★ **How:**

C. **Fill in the diagram with words to describe the dog, words to describe the wolf, and words to describe them both.**

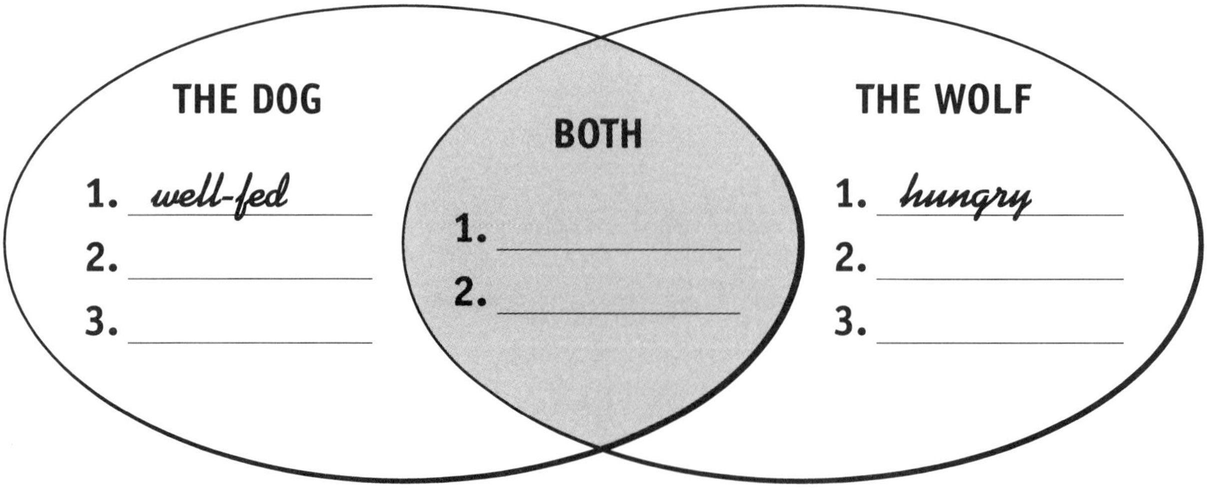

THE DOG
1. *well-fed*
2. ___
3. ___

BOTH
1. ___
2. ___

THE WOLF
1. *hungry*
2. ___
3. ___

UNIT 1: READING

Section 1: Types of Readings

📕 **Chapter 2:** Fiction and Poetry

📕 **Chapter 3:** Nonfiction

Section 2: Types of Questions

📕 **Chapter 4:** Answering Multiple-Choice Questions

📕 **Chapter 5:** Answering Open-Ended Questions

📕 **Chapter 6:** Checking Your Understanding

This part of the book focuses on preparing you for the **Fourth Grade Proficiency Test in Reading.** The reading selections on the test will be of two main types: (1) fiction / poetry; and (2) nonfiction. There will be several passages of each type. In addition, there will be 35 multiple-choice questions. These questions will emphasize critical thinking skills, not simply recalling information. This unit will help you to prepare for the reading test.

Chapter 2

FICTION AND POETRY

The Fourth Grade Proficiency Test in Reading will test your ability to read. Reading is a skill in which you connect words on a page with ideas and pictures in your head. As with every skill, you need to master some special techniques in order to become a good reader.

On the test there will be two main types of texts for you to read — fiction/poetry and nonfiction. This chapter focuses on fiction and poetry. **Fiction** is something that is made up by the author. It may be based on real facts, but the author has added an element of make-believe. There are many types of fiction, including stories, legends, poems, novels, and plays.

STORIES

Authors write stories to entertain, persuade or inform. Good stories can make us laugh or cry, or make our hearts pound with excitement. They help us use our imagination to understand how other people may feel in situations different from our own.

THE ELEMENTS OF A STORY

Just as every house has a floor and a roof, every good story is made up of different elements that the story-writer must bring together. These elements of a story are known as:

Let's look at a well-known story from Aesop's Fables to illustrate the elements of a story: *The Hare and the Tortoise*. A **hare** is a rabbit, while a **tortoise** is similar to a turtle except that it lives only on land.

THE HARE AND THE TORTOISE

A hare was making fun of a tortoise one day for being so slow. "Do you ever get anywhere?" the hare asked with a mocking laugh.

"Yes," replied the tortoise, "and I get there sooner than you think. I'll run you a race and prove it."

The hare was very amused at the thought of running a race with the tortoise, and just for fun he decided to do it. So the fox, who agreed to act as judge, marked the distance for the race on a path through the woods, and started the runners off.

The hare was soon far out of sight. To let the tortoise know how silly it was for him to challenge a speedy hare, the hare decided to lie down beside the path to take a nap until the tortoise could catch up.

The tortoise meanwhile kept going slowly but steadily. After a time, the tortoise passed the place where the hare was sleeping. The hare slept on very peacefully. When at last he did wake up, the tortoise was already very near the finish line. The hare now ran his swiftest, but he could not overtake the tortoise in time.

Now that you have read the story, let's examine each of its parts.

THE STORY SETTING

The story setting is **when** and **where** the story takes place. Often, the writer provides clues to indicate the story's time and place. For example, the language of the characters, their dress, or a description of where they are helps the reader to know the time period and place of the story.

A setting can be in the past, present, or future, or even in an imaginary world where time seems hardly to exist. Sometimes a tale may start with "Once upon a time" to indicate a make-believe setting.

The setting also includes the mood or tone of the story. It might be happy or sad, adventurous or romantic. Sometimes, the setting does not affect events in the story. At other times, the setting is important and influences what happens in the story.

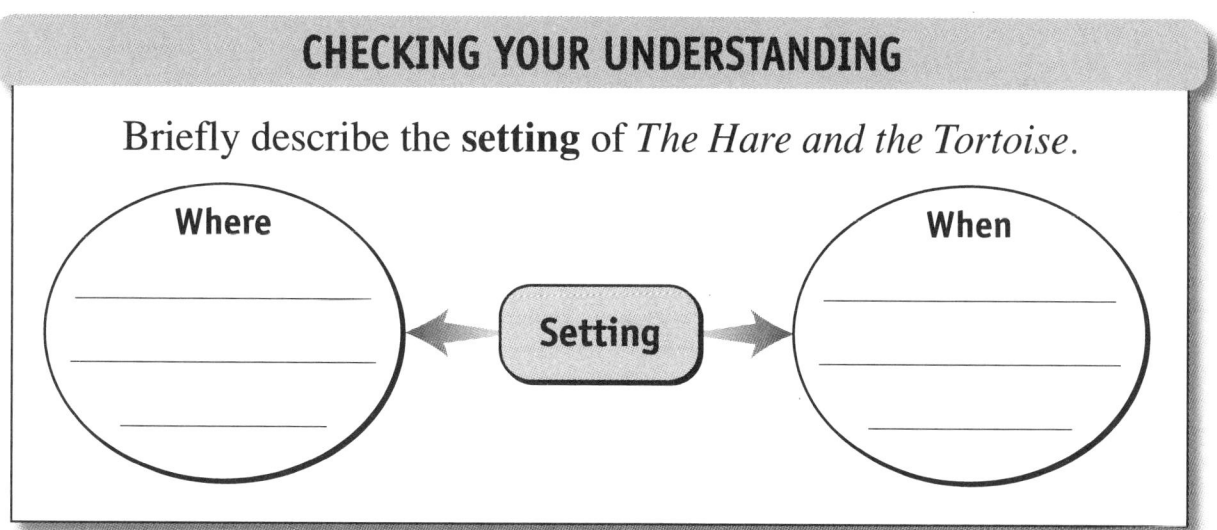

CHECKING YOUR UNDERSTANDING

Briefly describe the **setting** of *The Hare and the Tortoise*.

THE STORY CHARACTERS

The characters of a story are **who** the story is about. Characters are usually make-believe people but they may be real people in a make-believe setting. Story characters might even be animals or objects that act like people. In *The Hare and the Tortoise,* for example, the main characters are two animals that talk and act like people.

Most stories have only one or two main characters. The action in the story usually revolves around them. In *The Hare and the Tortoise,* we learn that the hare is fast. He thinks that because he is fast, he can make fun of the slow tortoise. When reading or listening to a story, think about how the author describes the characters:

★ **What do they look like?**

★ **How do they act?**

★ **What do they say?**

★ **How do they think and feel?**

★ **How do the characters change as the story unfolds?**

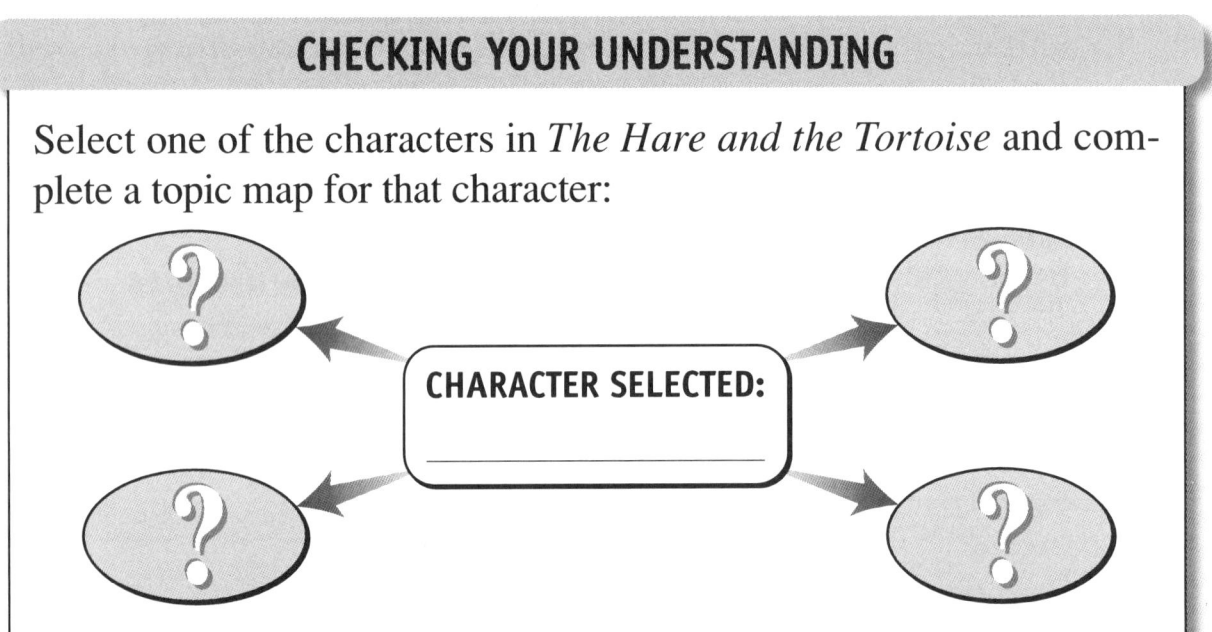

CHECKING YOUR UNDERSTANDING

Select one of the characters in *The Hare and the Tortoise* and complete a topic map for that character:

CHARACTER SELECTED: _____

THE STORY PLOT

The story plot refers to **what** takes place as the story unfolds. In most stories, the main characters face some obstacles or problems. Sometimes the main character has a **conflict** with another character. In other stories, the main character faces an internal conflict — such as having to make a difficult decision. The plot is made up of a series of events in which the characters try to deal with these problems and conflicts.

An author usually tries to maintain the reader's interest in the story by creating some kind of suspense. As the plot unfolds, new twists arise making the main problem worse. The reader wants to continue reading the story to find out how these problems are solved. The story ends when the main characters solve their problems or learn to accept them.

To keep track of the plot, it helps to use a sequence map. For example, let's create one for *The Hare and the Tortoise*. The sequence map has already been started for you. Complete the remaining boxes:

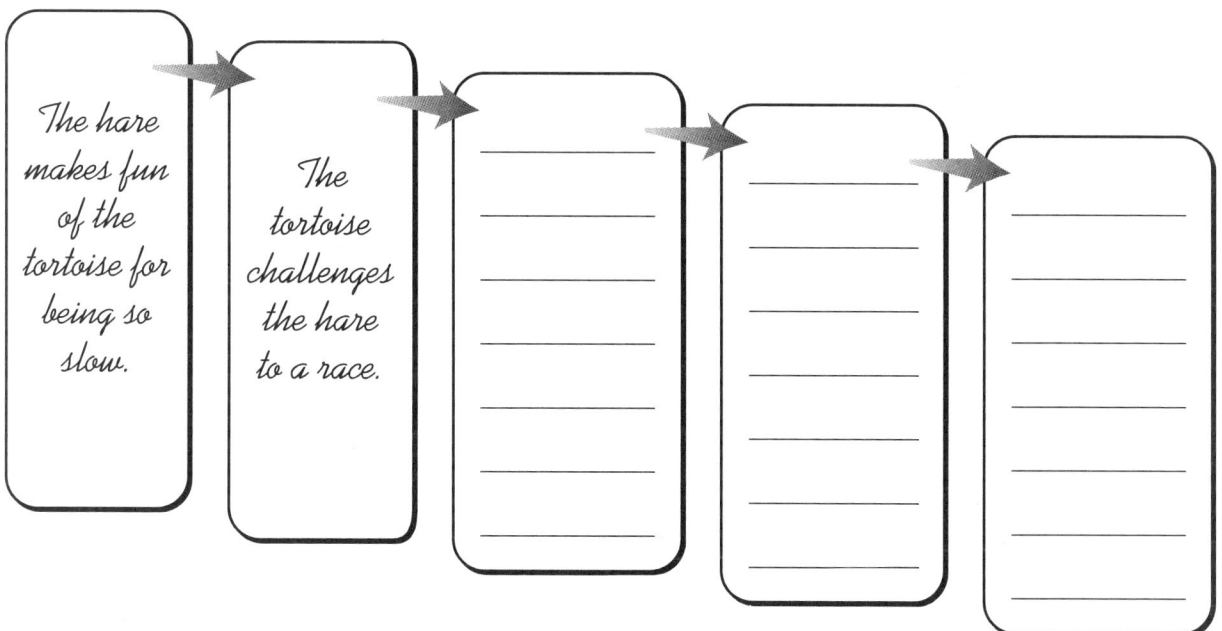

THE STORY THEME OR LESSON

Stories often interest us because they teach us a message or lesson we can apply in our own lives. This message or lesson is called the theme of the story. A story may have one or more themes. The theme is why the story is important. For example, in *The Hare and the Tortoise,* one lesson is that being over-confident can lead to failure.

CHECKING YOUR UNDERSTANDING

Briefly describe another **theme** of *The Hare and the Tortoise*.

POETRY

In addition to reading a story, you may be asked to read and interpret a poem on the **Fourth Grade Proficiency Test in Reading.** Like a story, many poems have a setting, characters, a plot, and a theme. However, not all poems tell stories. Some poems simply describe something — such as a beautiful flower, the arrival of spring, or the poet's feelings of love.

THE CHARACTERISTICS OF POETRY

Although there are several types of poetry, most poems share certain characteristics.

★ **Rhythm.** When you read a poem, the syllables are usually arranged so that you can hear a strong beat. It is almost like reading to the beat of a drum.

★ **Imagery.** Poets make use of appealing images or word pictures to express feelings and ideas. They use language to create a word picture. Two main types are simile and metaphor. A **simile** uses *like* or *as* to make a comparison: "Her eyes twinkled like stars." A **metaphor** makes a comparison without like or as: "The sun was a glowing red ball."

★ **Rhyme and other sound patterns.** Many poems are written so that a word or line ends in the same last sound as another word or line. Poets also use other sound patterns to give poetry a musical quality. For example, they may use a series of words that begin with the same sound, like "soft as skin." This is known as **alliteration.**

ANALYZING POETRY

The first thing you should decide when reading a poem is whether the poem tells a story or describes something. If the poet tells a story, then try to keep track of all the story elements, just like any other story. For other poems, identify what the poet is describing and the poet's feelings about it.

Let's look at a typical poem. As you can see, instead of full sentences, poetry is organized by lines. When reading a poem, the reader usually pauses at the end of each line. Several lines of poetry are organized into something similar to paragraphs, known as **stanzas.** The poem *Whispers* has three stanzas. After reading the poem, analyze it by completing the box below.

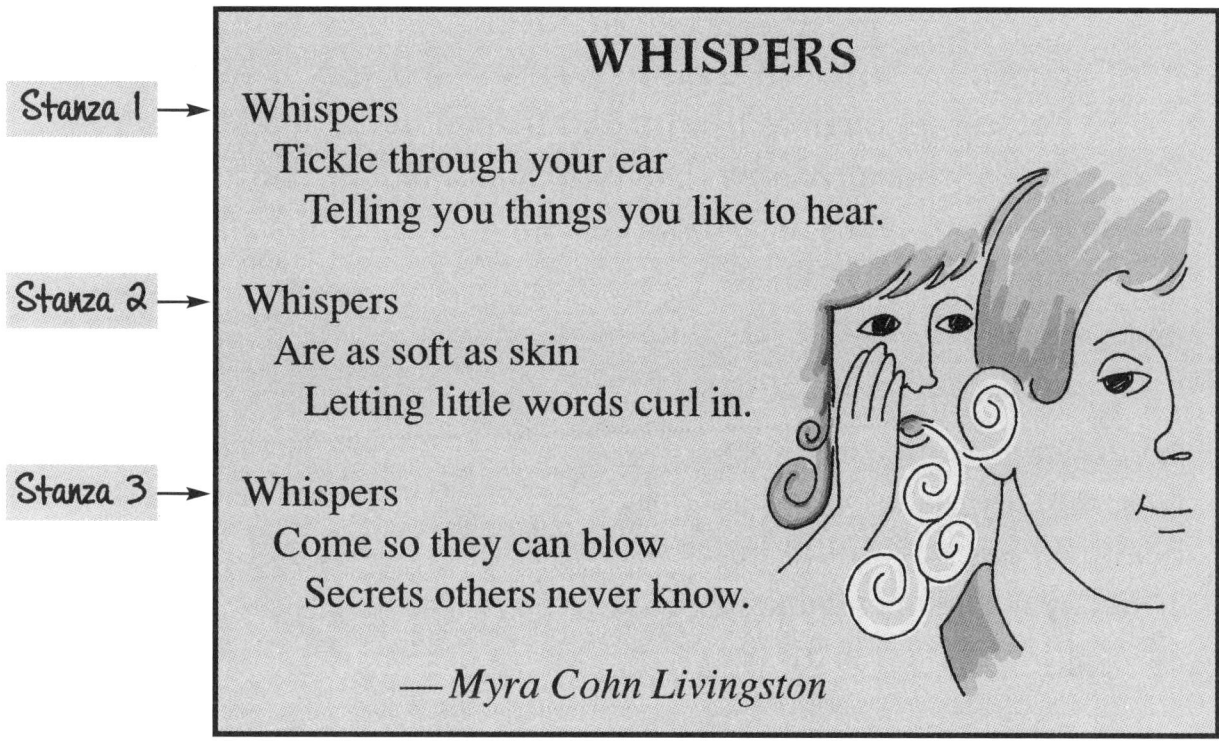

ANALYZING A POEM

What is the poem mostly about? _____

_____

What are the poet's feeling about this topic? _____

_____

How does this poem make you feel? Use the poem to explain why you feel this way. _____

_____

Practice Exercises

Directions: Read the story below and complete one of the graphic organizers that follow.

THE SHOEMAKER AND THE ELVES

There once was a shoemaker who worked very hard, but could not earn enough to live on. All he had in the world was gone, except enough leather to make one last pair of shoes. He cut the leather into a pattern to make into shoes the next day and then went to bed.

In the morning, when he sat down to work, the shoes were already made — and as beautiful as they could be. That day a customer came in and paid a high price for the shoes.

The poor shoemaker then bought enough leather to make two more pairs. In the evening, he cut out the patterns again and went to bed.

When he got up the next morning, the shoes were again finished. Two buyers came in, and they, too, paid him well for the shoes. So he now bought leather for four pairs. Again, he cut the leather at night and found new shoes finished in the morning. This went on for some time, and the shoemaker became successful again.

One evening the shoemaker said to his wife, "I want to stay up and watch who comes and does my work for me." So he and his wife hid behind a curtain and watched to see what would happen.

continued

At midnight, two little elves sat down at his bench and began to work, quickly stitching and tapping away. When the elves finished, they ran off, as quick as lightning.

The next day his wife said, "These elves have made us rich. We ought to do them a good deed in return. They must be cold, running about with hardly anything on. I will make each of them a shirt, a coat, a vest, and a pair of pants. You make each of them a little pair of shoes." The shoemaker agreed.

When all the things were ready, he and his wife laid them on the table. Then they went and hid behind the curtain.

At midnight, the elves came in to work as usual when they saw the clothes. They laughed in surprise as they dressed themselves in the twinkling of an eye. Then they danced around the room and out the door.

The shoemaker never saw them again, but everything went well with him from that time forward.

There are many ways to graphically organize material about a story. On the following pages are two suggested ways of making a graphic organizer. Select **one** of these and complete the needed information.

STORY MAPPING: TYPE #1

TITLE: _____

SETTING:

★ Where: _____

★ When: _____

MAIN CHARACTERS:

★ Who: _____

★ Who: _____

PLOT: *(List the events in the order that they happened)*

❶ _____

❷ _____

❸ _____

❹ _____

❺ _____

THEME OR LESSON:

★ _____

★ _____

STORY MAPPING: TYPE #2

The Setting

Characters: _____

Place: _____

The Problem

_____

The Goal

_____

Event 1 _____

_____

Event 2 _____

_____

Event 3 _____

_____

Event 4 _____

_____

The Resolution

_____

_____

Directions: Read the following poem and then complete the box that follows:

SEA CALM

How still,
How strangely still
The water is today.
It is not good
For water,
To be so still that way.

— *Langston Hughes*

ANALYZING A POEM

What is the poem mostly about? _____

_____

What are the poet's feeling about this topic? _____

_____

How does this poem make you feel? Use the poem to explain why

you feel this way. _____

_____

CHAPTER 3

NONFICTION

In addition to fiction and poetry, the **Fourth Grade Proficiency Test in Reading** will test your ability to read nonfiction. **Nonfiction** is any reading passage attempting to tell the truth about real people, events and things. The aim of the author is generally to inform the reader. Some people refer to nonfiction as **informational.**

THE TOPIC SENTENCE

Writers of nonfiction usually organize their ideas about a topic into separate paragraphs. A paragraph is a group of sentences that tell about the same thing. Each paragraph will usually have its own topic sentence. The **topic sentence** generally identifies what the paragraph is about. The topic sentence is often more general than the rest of the paragraph. If we look only at the topic sentences for all of the paragraphs of a nonfiction text, we can often figure out the writer's main ideas about the topic. Remember, only one sentence in each paragraph is a topic sentence.

SUPPORTING DETAILS

Just identifying the topic sentence of a paragraph is not enough. It is simply the first step in understanding what the paragraph is about. The rest of the paragraph explains the topic sentence and gives supporting details. The detail sentences support the topic sentence by giving us more information about it.

It is sometimes easy to "see" how information is organized by creating a graphic organizer. Look at the following paragraph to see how details in an informational paragraph support the topic sentence:

> Where people live usually affects how they live. People who live in warm climates wear light clothing. People who live in cold climates wear several layers of clothing. Homes in warm climates are made of lighter materials than those in cold climates.

Let's use this paragraph to make a graphic organizer.

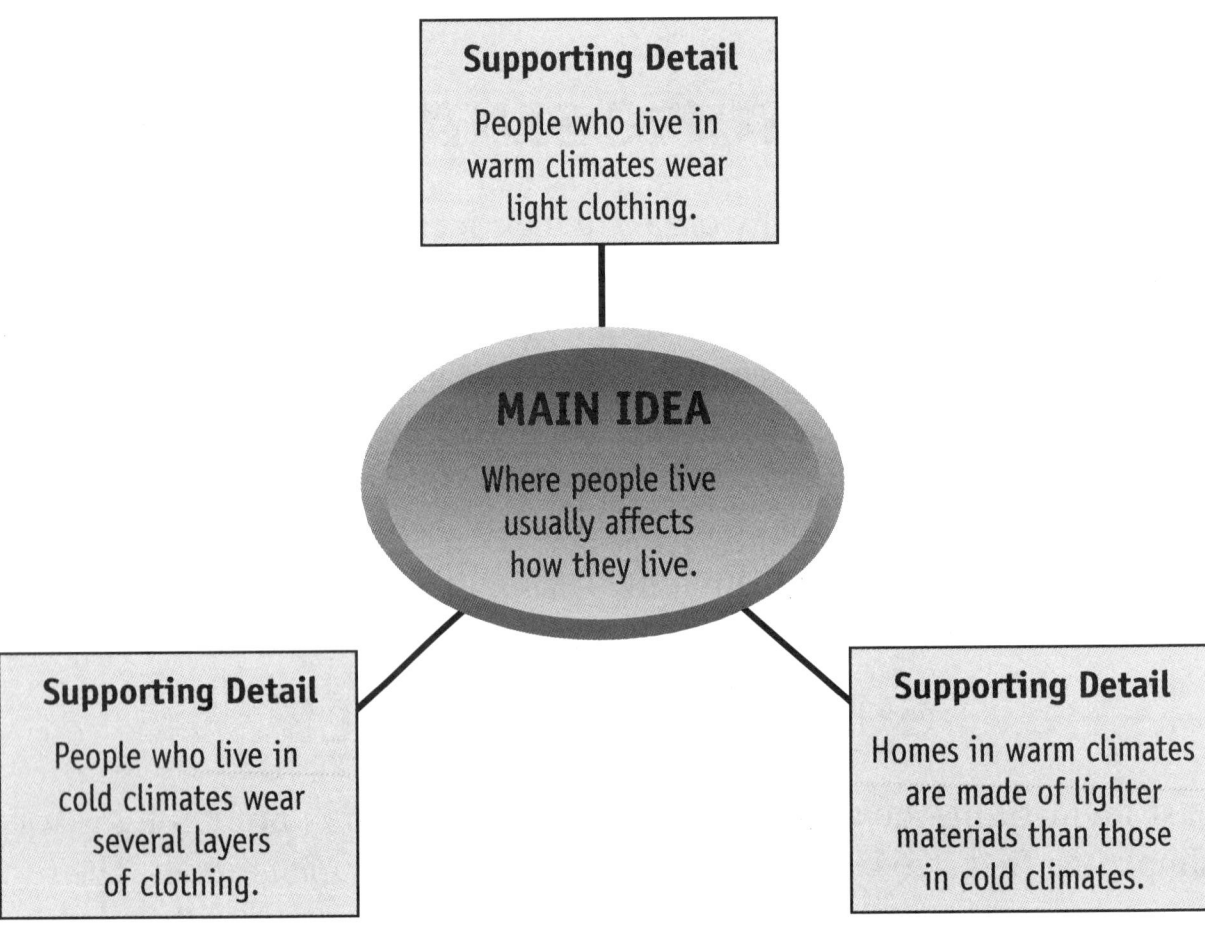

Notice how each supporting detail is a specific example illustrating the topic sentence — that where people live affects how they live.

FINDING THE MAIN IDEA

The **main idea** of a reading selection tells what the selection is mostly about. To find the main idea of a nonfiction reading, take the following two steps:

STEP 1: Determine the topic of the reading.

In this first step, try to identify the subject of the reading. Ask yourself, "What is this selection mostly about?" Is it about climate? Is it about the location of cities? The topic should be general enough to cover all the details in the reading.

STEP 2: Determine what the writer is saying about the topic.

Once you have identified the topic of a reading, focus on what the author is saying about it. Is the author giving you the *who, what, where, when, why,* and *how?* What does the author say about each of these? Or does the author have a single message he or she is trying to send to the reader? The answers to these questions will guide you to the main idea of the reading.

Often, the main idea of an informational reading is stated at the beginning of the reading in a **thesis statement.** This is a brief statement of one or two sentences in which the author tells the reader what he or she is trying to show, explain, describe, or demonstrate.

Practice Exercises

Directions: In the following reading, you will be asked to identify the main idea, the topic sentences, and one of the supporting details.

The American Civil War

Most historians agree that there were several causes of the Civil War. Many think the most important cause of the Civil War was slavery. In the North, the economy was based on free laborers. In Southern states, plantation owners used slaves to grow cotton and other crops. Slaves were not free and did not receive any wages. They were often mistreated by their owners. Northern abolitionists wanted to end slavery. Slave owners argued that their slaves were better treated than many factory workers in the North.

A Slave Auction

Another cause of the Civil War was the concern in the North and South about the spread of slavery into new states in the West. Northerners and Southerners disagreed over whether these new states should permit slavery. In 1860, Abraham Lincoln was elected President. Lincoln opposed the spread of slavery to new states.

A third cause of the war was a disagreement over states' rights. Some Americans believed each state had a right to secede (*withdraw*) from the United States if it wished. After Lincoln was elected, several Southern states decided to secede. President Lincoln called for volunteers to fight against those states that had seceded.

CHAPTER 3: NONFICTION   **31**

Main Idea of the Reading: _____
_____

Paragraph 1: Its Topic Sentence: _____
_____

A Supporting Detail for that Topic Sentence: _____
_____

Paragraph 2: Its Topic Sentence: _____
_____

A Supporting Detail for that Topic Sentence: _____
_____

Paragraph 3: Its Topic Sentence: _____
_____

A Supporting Detail for that Topic Sentence: _____
_____

Directions: Use the reading about Beijing to complete the graphic organizer below.

BEIJING

Beijing (bay-jing) is one of the world's most important cities. Located at about the same latitude as New York City, the city became the capital of China in 1279. In the 1400s, Chinese emperors built a large network of palaces known as the Forbidden City, at the center of Beijing. Home to the rulers of China for the next five hundred years, the Forbidden City was looked upon as the center of the universe.

In 1911, the emperor was overthrown, and China became a republic. In 1928, the ruling Nationalist Party renamed the old imperial city Beiping, a word that means "peace." When the Communists came to power in 1949, they restored the traditional name of Beijing, meaning "northern capital," and made it their capital.

Under Communist rule, Beijing's rundown appearance was changed. Beijing became a city of well-paved streets. Slums were torn down and government buildings, hotels and offices were constructed. Today, Beijing remains the capital of China. More than 13 million people live in this busy capital. The city's art treasures and architectural monuments continue to attract millions of foreign visitors each year.

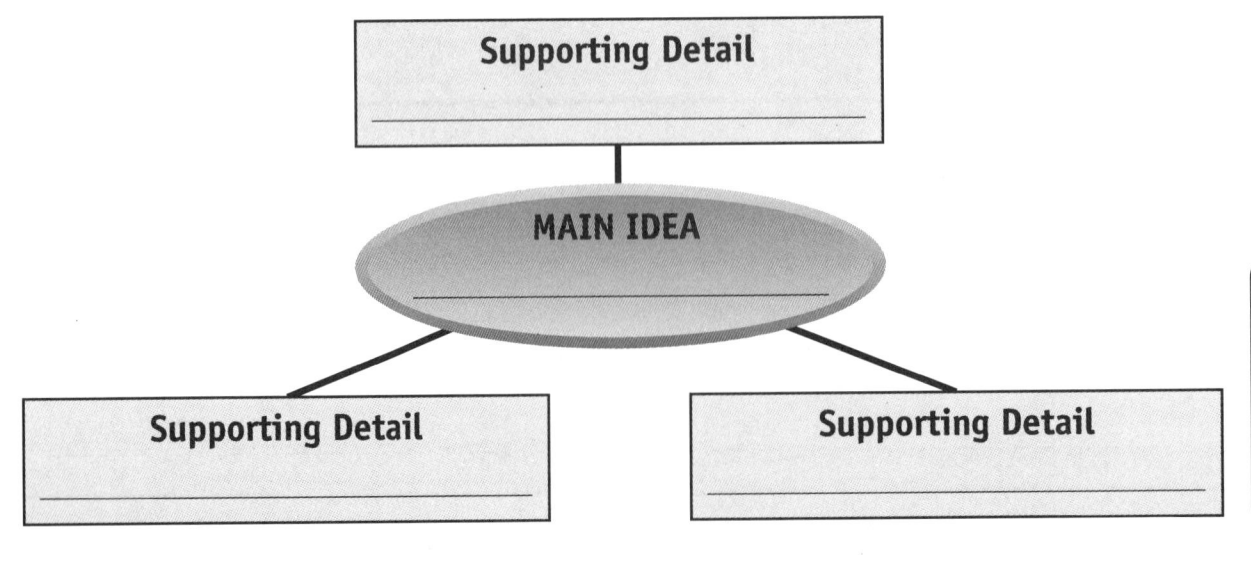

Supporting Detail
_____

MAIN IDEA
_____

Supporting Detail
_____

Supporting Detail
_____

CHAPTER 4

ANSWERING MULTIPLE-CHOICE QUESTIONS

The **Fourth Grade Proficiency Test in Reading** will consist of several reading passages. Each reading selection is followed by a series of questions. Some of these will be multiple-choice. Each multiple-choice question will have three possible choices. Your task will be to select the best of the three choices to answer the question.

The multiple-choice questions on the test can be grouped into two main types:

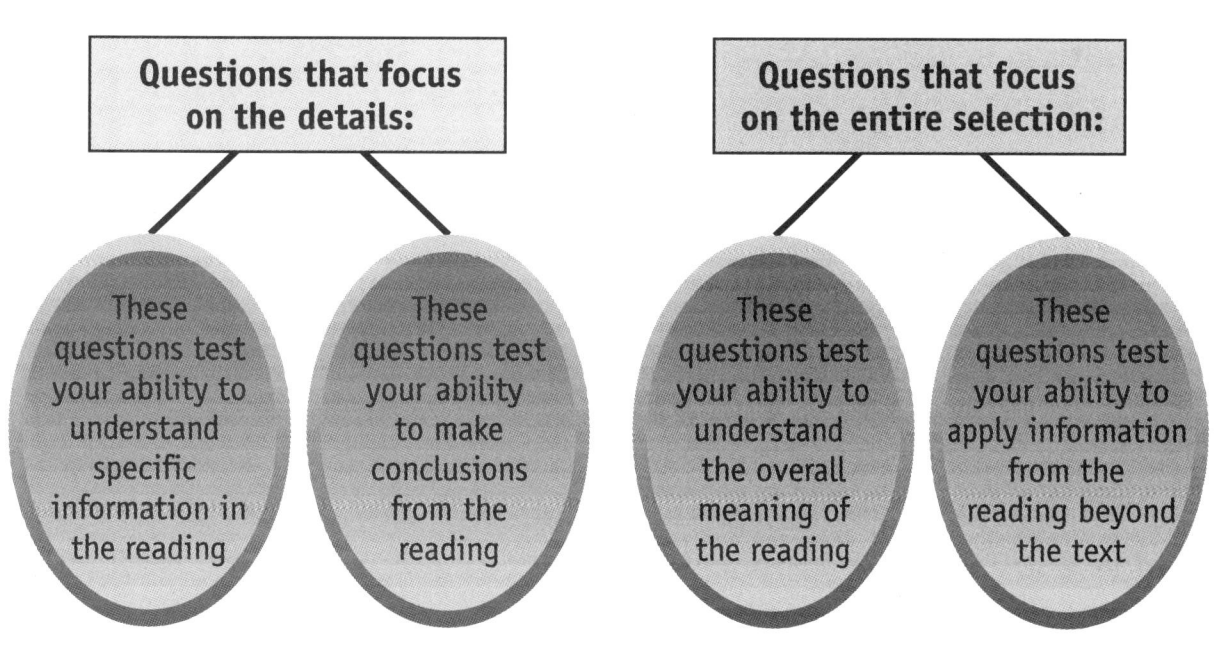

Questions that focus on the details:
- These questions test your ability to understand specific information in the reading
- These questions test your ability to make conclusions from the reading

Questions that focus on the entire selection:
- These questions test your ability to understand the overall meaning of the reading
- These questions test your ability to apply information from the reading beyond the text

This chapter examines each of these types of questions and how they might appear on Ohio's **Fourth Grade Proficiency Test in Reading.**

TOPIC QUESTIONS

Topic questions test whether you understand the main topic of an entire passage. Think of the main topic as similar to a newspaper headline. A headline gives you a general idea of what a news article is about.

The answers to *topic questions* focus on summarizing what the whole reading is about. Try to think of a single sentence or statement that sums up what the whole passage or story is mostly about. For informational texts, this is the main idea of the reading. The title and illustrations may provide helpful clues. Any choices that focus only on specific details rather than the whole story are probably not the right answer.

Let's practice answering *topic questions*. Read the passage below and answer the question that follows:

> A poor fisherman, who lived on the fish he caught, one day caught only a small fish. He was about to put it in his basket when the little fish spoke up. "Please spare me, Mr. Fisherman. I am so small it isn't worthwhile to carry me home. When I'm bigger, I will make you a much better meal." The fisherman quickly put the fish into his basket. "How foolish I would be," he said, "to throw you back. However small you are, you are better than nothing."

1 Which sentence best tells the main idea of this selection?
   ○ **A** Catching fish is often difficult.
   ○ **B** There was a fisherman who did not trust fish that talked.
   ○ **C** A fisherman decided a small fish was better than none.

CHECKING YOUR UNDERSTANDING

What is the answer to **Question 1**? _____ Explain your answer.

_____

_____

COMPREHENSION QUESTIONS

Comprehension questions test how well you understand a reading selection. They usually ask you to identify important details in the reading. There are a variety of ways in which *comprehension questions* may appear on the test. Four of the most common are identified below.

DETAIL QUESTIONS

Detail questions focus on the details of a reading — the *who, what, when, where,* and *how* of what takes place. *Detail questions* following a story will usually ask for specific details about the story's setting, characters and events. If the reading is nonfiction, *detail questions* will focus on important supporting details and facts found in the text. Either way, answers to detail questions are usually found **directly** in the reading.

If you do not recall what the answer to the question is, you should **scan** the reading. To *scan* is to read through the text quickly for particular information. One way to scan is to look for **key words.** For example, if a question asks about a particular character or event in a story, you should look through the passage quickly until your eyes spot the name of the character or event you need.

Let's practice answering *detail questions*. Read the passage at the top of the next page and answer the questions that follow:

One day, ten-year old Carmen Hernandez woke up late for school. She wasn't feeling well and started to sweat. Her mother called her for breakfast, but the thought of eating oatmeal made Carmen feel even sicker. Her mother came into her bedroom and took her temperature. After a few moments, she read the thermometer. "Carmen, my dear," she said. "You have a high fever. I think you have the flu!"

2   **What was Carmen supposed to have for breakfast that morning?**
   ○ A   oatmeal
   ○ B   waffles
   ○ C   pancakes

3   **What did Carmen's mother think was wrong with Carmen?**
   ○ A   She forgot to eat breakfast.
   ○ B   She had too much to eat the night before.
   ○ C   She was sick with the flu.

CHECKING YOUR UNDERSTANDING

What is the answer to **Question 2**? _____ Copy the sentence where you found your answer. _____

What is the answer to **Question 3**? _____ Explain your answer.

_____

Sometimes, a *detail question* may ask you to complete a **concept map** or other **graphic organizer.** Such questions are another way of asking a multiple-choice question.

To answer such a question, simply pick the word that best fits into the empty box. For example, using the story about Carmen, answer the following question:

4 Which word would best fit in Box 1?
  ○ **A** hungry
  ○ **B** happy
  ○ **C** sick

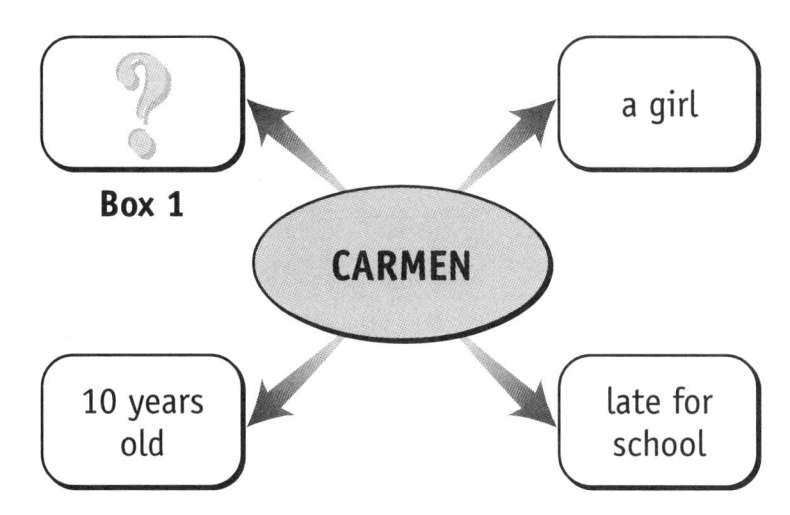

Later on in this book, you will learn about other types of questions that might appear as graphic organizers.

CHECKING YOUR UNDERSTANDING

What is the answer to **Question 4**? _____ Explain your answer.

_____

SEQUENCE QUESTIONS

Sequence questions test your ability to follow the plot of a story or a series of events described in a reading. These questions examine your ability to describe the order in which the events happened. For example, you may be asked what happened *before or after* an event in the story, or you may be asked to identify which list of events is in the correct order.

The answers to *sequence questions* will usually be found directly in the reading. Certain key words and phrases in a reading often indicate that things are happening in sequence. Clues to the sequence of events are found in key words like *after, before, since, last* and *first*.

Let's practice answering *sequence questions*. Read the passage below and answer the questions that follow:

> Matt was becoming concerned. He had to buy a birthday gift for Steve, but he still didn't have any idea what to get. So Matt phoned Ross, who said that Steve loved watching basketball. After he spoke to Ross, Matt hurried to the ticket booth to buy a pair of tickets to next week's game. His smile turned to a frown when he saw a sign posted on the ticket booth stating that the whole season was already sold out.

By scanning the reading, you can see the following sequence:

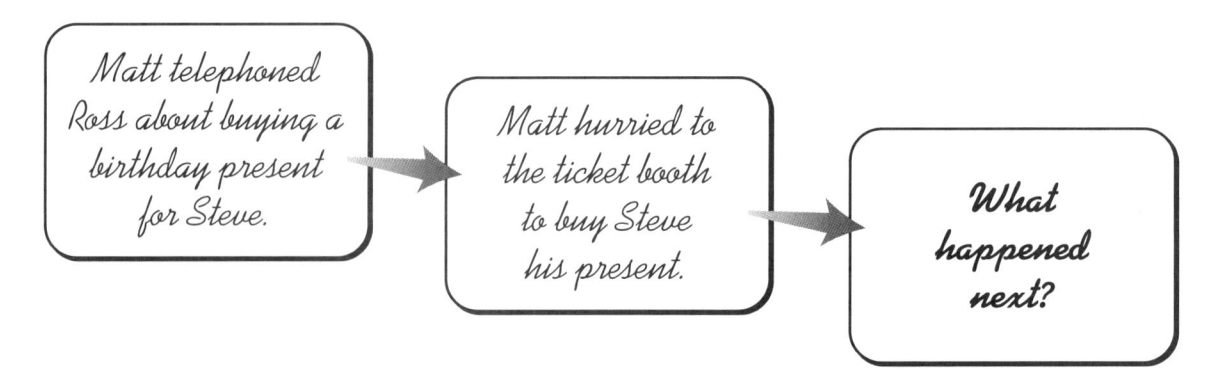

Matt telephoned Ross about buying a birthday present for Steve. → *Matt hurried to the ticket booth to buy Steve his present.* → *What happened next?*

5 What happened after Matt spoke to Ross?
  ○ A He was invited to Steve's birthday party.
  ○ B He decided not to go to the party.
  ○ C He hurried off to the ticket booth.

6 Which event in the story happened first?
  ○ A Matt telephoned Ross.
  ○ B Matt was unable to buy tickets.
  ○ C Matt went to the ticket booth.

CHECKING YOUR UNDERSTANDING

What is the answer to **Question 5**? _____ Copy the sentence where you found your answer. _____

What is the answer to **Question 6**? _____ Explain your answer.
_____

EXPLANATION QUESTIONS

Explanation questions test your understanding of the relationship between the **cause** of an action or event and its **effect** — what happened *as a result of* the action or event.

★ The **cause** of something is *why something happened*. For example, turning on a light switch allows electricity to flow to the bulb and lights it up. Your turn of the switch was the *cause* of the light's going on.

★ An **effect** is what happens *because* of a situation, action or event. For example, the light's going on was the *effect* of your turn of the switch. Sometimes a single cause can set in motion a whole chain of effects.

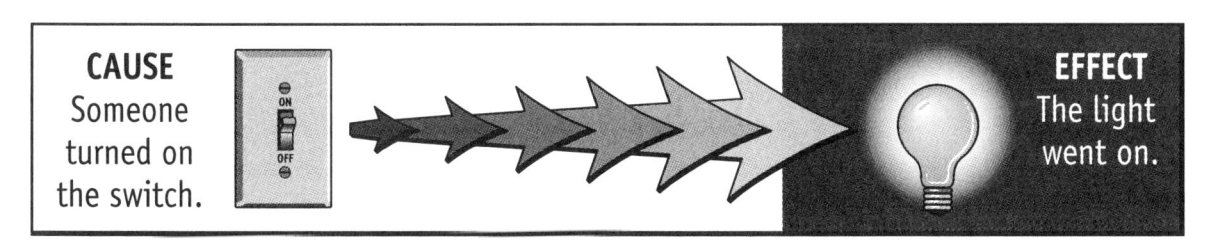

CAUSE Someone turned on the switch. → **EFFECT** The light went on.

The answers to *explanation questions* will usually be found directly in the reading. The passage will tell you that one event caused another. There are several key words or phrases in a reading that may indicate cause and effect. Look for key words such as *because, as a result of, since, due to, so,* and *on account of.* Sometimes you will not find these words but it will still be clear from the reading that one event caused another.

Let's practice answering *explanation questions*. Read the passage below and answer the questions that follow:

A bull once escaped from a lion by entering a cave used by goat herders to house their flocks in stormy weather. It happened that one of the goats was still in the cave. The bull no sooner got inside than the goat rushed him, butting him with his horns. The impact sent the bull crashing into the wall. Because the lion was still prowling outside the cave's entrance, the bull had to submit to the insult. "Do not think," the bull said, "that I submit to your treatment because I am afraid of you. When the lion leaves, I'll teach you a lesson you won't forget."

7 **Why did the bull flee into the cave?**
   ◯ **A** The bull was tired from working all day.
   ◯ **B** The bull feared being attacked by the lion.
   ◯ **C** The bull lived in the cave.

8 **What was the result of the goat's butting the bull with his horns?**
   ◯ **A** The bull crashed into the wall.
   ◯ **B** The bull threatened the lion.
   ◯ **C** The lion attacked the goat.

CHECKING YOUR UNDERSTANDING

What is the answer to **Question 7**? _____ Copy the sentence where you found your answer. _____

What is the answer to **Question 8**? _____ Copy the sentence where you found your answer. _____

COMPARE-AND-CONTRAST QUESTIONS

We often compare and contrast things to better understand each of them. You have already learned how to compare and contrast items to complete a Venn diagram. You may also have a multiple-choice question that requires you to compare and contrast two characters or other story elements.

The answers to *compare-and-contrast questions* will usually be found directly in the reading selection. Go back to the section of the passage describing the items you are comparing, and see what these items have in common and what is different about each of them. After you have done this, you are then ready to answer the question. Let's practice answering *compare-and-contrast questions*.

> After the Civil War, Ohio became a major center for manufacturing. Benjamin F. Goodrich opened his first rubber manufacturing plant in Akron, Ohio, in 1870. John D. Rockefeller of Cleveland, Ohio, started a company in the 1870s that brought crude oil from Pennsylvania to Ohio, where it was refined. Rockefeller's business soon became the world's largest oil company, making Rockefeller one of the world's richest and most powerful men.

9 In what way were Benjamin F. Goodrich and John D. Rockefeller similar?

○ **A** They both started oil companies.
○ **B** They both started industries in Ohio.
○ **C** They both brought raw materials from Pennsylvania.

CHECKING YOUR UNDERSTANDING

What is the answer to **Question 9**? _____ Explain your answer.

VOCABULARY QUESTIONS

Vocabulary questions test your understanding of how a word or phrase is used in a specific place in a reading. Sometimes you may come across a word that you don't know. Other times, you may find a word or phrase that has several meanings. You must decide which meaning most closely agrees with the way the word or phrase is used in the reading.

To answer this kind of question, you should use **context clues** to help you figure out the exact meaning of the word or expression. Think of yourself as a detective. The surrounding words, phrases, and sentences provide clues that help you determine the meaning of the word or phrase.

Here are some techniques to help you with *vocabulary questions:*

★ **Examine Nearby Sentences.** You can often determine the meaning of a word or phrase by examining another part of the passage. It sometimes helps to read the sentence before or after the word or phrase in question. These sentences often contain clues about the vocabulary meaning.

★ **Analyze the Unfamiliar Word.** If a word is unfamiliar to you, think of words that you already know that look like the word. Similar words allow you to figure out the unknown word's meaning. Try to figure out the word by breaking it apart — look at the way the word starts, the base word or root of the word, and the way it ends.

★ **Substitute Vocabulary from the Question Choices.** Try substituting each of the choices provided by the question and choose the word or phrase that makes the most sense in the sentence.

Let's practice answering *vocabulary questions*. Read the passage on the next page and answer the question that follows:

CHAPTER 4: ANSWERING MULTIPLE-CHOICE QUESTIONS   43

> The mayor called together the town council for an emergency meeting. It was nearly September, and the new school was still not completed. "We must pay the builders a supplement[1] to work on weekends until the job is done," the mayor announced. Everyone stood and applauded this suggestion. By ten o'clock that evening, all other issues had been dealt with and the meeting was ready to **adjourn.** The members of the council and the mayor grabbed their umbrellas and jackets and dashed out into the pouring rain.
>
> ---
> [1] more money

Whenever you see a footnote explaining a word, read the passage as though the word or phrase at the bottom of the page was substituted in place of the difficult word.

10 In the passage, the meeting was ready to *adjourn* at ten o'clock. What does *adjourn* mean?
   - **A** continue
   - **B** end
   - **C** postpone

CHECKING YOUR UNDERSTANDING

What is the answer to **Question 10**? _____ Explain your answer.

_____
_____

INFERENTIAL QUESTIONS

Inferential questions require you to *infer* or figure out answers from clues in the passage and from your own experience. Inferential questions ask you to go beyond what is written directly in the reading. Inferential questions ask you to add your own thinking to what you learned from the text. Let's look at some types of inferential questions you might find on the test.

DRAWING-CONCLUSION QUESTIONS

Drawing-conclusion questions ask you to pull together details in the reading. The key to answering this type of question is to find specific things or events in the reading to use as clues. Then apply your thinking skills to identify the right answer.

If a question asks what word best describes a character, you need to:

★ **review** the different actions taken by that character.

★ **identify** a word that best expresses the qualities of that character.

★ **decide** which word from the choices given in the question best summarizes those actions or expresses those qualities.

If a question asks you *who* is telling the story, you need to:

★ **look** carefully at the clues found in the story. For example, if the pronoun "I" is being used, who is speaking?

★ **determine** the point of view from which the story is being told. If the storyteller is describing the actions of others, it may be an outside narrator telling the story, rather than one of the characters.

Let's practice answering some *drawing-conclusion questions*. Read the passage on the next page and answer the questions that follow:

A young boy put his hand into a cookie jar to get out some cookies. He took such a large fistful of cookies that he could not withdraw his hand. There the young boy stood, unwilling to give up even a single cookie, yet unable to get all the cookies in his hand out at once. Soon he began to cry. "My boy," said his mother, "be satisfied with half the cookies in your hand and you will easily get your hand out. Then perhaps you may have some more cookies later."

11 **Which word best describes the young boy?**
   - **A** loyal
   - **B** greedy
   - **C** happy

12 **Who is telling this story?**
   - **A** the boy
   - **B** his mother
   - **C** a narrator

CHECKING YOUR UNDERSTANDING

What is the answer to **Question 11**? _____ Explain your answer.

_____

What is the answer to **Question 12**? _____ Explain your answer.

_____

PREDICTION QUESTIONS

Can you predict the future? Maybe not, but *prediction questions* call on your ability to forecast or *predict* what a character would probably do in a particular situation or what might happen next in a particular reading.

Prediction questions may even ask you to take specific things described in the reading and to apply them in a new way. For example, a character may have showed kindness in a story. A *prediction question* might ask you to show how that character would behave in a new situation. You should select the answer that shows the character acting in a similar way.

Let's practice answering prediction questions. Read the passage below and answer the question that follows:

> Samuel was learning to become a carpenter. One day he was sent to buy some supplies. Everyone in the store that day was quite excited. People were arguing and shouting at each other. News had just arrived that some American colonists up north had opened fire on British troops at Lexington and Concord. Samuel became excited, too. He told the storekeeper that it was about time the colonists did something. He felt that the colonies in America were far too big to be ruled by a distant, tiny island like Great Britain.
>
> *Colonists stop to talk in front of a store.*

13 **If asked whether the American colonies should pay more taxes to Great Britain, how might Samuel respond?**
  ○ **A** No, because the Southern colonists did not have to pay taxes.
  ○ **B** Yes, because the American colonists were loyal British subjects.
  ○ **C** No, because the American colonists should be independent of Great Britain.

★ **Almanac.** An *almanac* is a book of facts. A new edition is published every year, so it is always up to date. Almanacs cover a wide range of subjects, such as current events and statistics. They often contain lists, such as Nobel prize winners, famous athletes, and information about sporting events, countries, cities, and astronomical bodies.

★ **Biography.** A *biography* is a book about a person's life. It usually tells the story of the person's life and accomplishments.

★ **Autobiography.** An *autobiography* is a book that a person writes about his or her own life.

In addition to specialized reference books, this kind of question may give you a list of book titles and ask you to select the book that is most likely to give you more information related to the reading. To answer this question, choose the title that is general enough to give you more information on the main topic of the reading. It should not be so specific that it just touches on one aspect of the reading.

Now using the story that you read on page 46, answer the following question:

14 Which book would give more information about the issues Samuel heard the colonists discussing?
○ A *The Story of America's Independence*
○ B *American Occupations*
○ C *The History of General Stores in America*

CHECKING YOUR UNDERSTANDING

What is the answer to **Question 14**? _____ Explain your answer.
_____
_____

CHECKING YOUR UNDERSTANDING

What is the answer to **Question 13**? _____ Explain your a____

_____

_____

LIBRARY RESOURCE QUESTIONS

Some questions will test your ability to identify library sources
materials you might use to find out more about the topic of the r
For these questions, you have to go beyond the text and use yo
outside knowledge to determine which additional material would l
helpful. To answer this kind of question, you should be familiar v
main reference tools located in your school or community library.

★ **Encyclopedia.** *Encyclopedias* have articles about cou
famous people, and other topics, arranged in alphabetical
Since encyclopedias cover such a wide range of topics, the
ally consist of many volumes.

★ **Dictionary.** A *dictionary* has a list of words and their defi
in alphabetical order. Usually, the pronunciation, spelling
of speech and definitions are provided for each word.

★ **Thesaurus.** A *thesaurus* is a book used by writers to fin
the right word or phrase. It lists words and phrases and
synonyms — other words with similar meaning.

★ **Atlas.** An *atlas* is a special book containing maps and other
mation about geography. Atlases may contain physical, poli
historical and other kinds of specialized maps.

THEME QUESTIONS

You already know that a story may have one or more themes. A theme is any underlying message or lesson that the story teaches. Sometimes a theme is mentioned directly in the story. At other times, you have to figure out the theme (or themes). A *theme question* asks you to determine the theme of a story. Think about a general message the story has that you could apply to your own life. To determine a story theme, ask yourself the following:

★ *What lesson can I learn from reading the story?*

— or —

★ *What advice does the author give to the reader?*

Let's practice answering *theme questions*. Read the passage below and answer the question that follows.

> Two travelers, walking in the noonday sun, sought the shade of a nearby tree to rest. As they lay looking up at the leaves, they saw that it was a maple tree. "How useless is this maple tree!" said one of them. "It bears no fruit whatever and only serves to litter the ground with its leaves." Suddenly a voice from the maple tree replied, "Ungrateful creatures! You lie here receiving the cooling shade I provide, yet you say I am useless! Instead, you should be grateful for the benefits you receive from me!"

15 What lesson can we learn from this story?
- ○ **A** Simple benefits are often the least appreciated.
- ○ **B** Trees without fruit are useless.
- ○ **C** There is nothing more enjoyable than a sunny day.

CHECKING YOUR UNDERSTANDING

What is the answer to **Question 15**? _____ Explain your answer.

_____

_____

_____

TEST-TAKING STRATEGIES

This section introduces a three-step approach you can use for reading a selection and answering the multiple-choice questions on the **Grade 4 Proficiency Test in Reading.**

STEP 1: IDENTIFY THE TYPE OF READING

Before reading the text, examine the title and any illustrations that might accompany the text. The title and illustrations will often give you a quick idea of what the reading is about. You can also skim through the reading itself to see how long it is and to get a sense of what it is about.

During your first look at the reading, you should quickly identify whether you are reading a story, poem, or nonfiction text.

STEP 2: READ WITH A PURPOSE

After you have identified the type of reading selection, you should read the passage carefully for detail. Reading with a purpose will help you to understand the passage more easily.

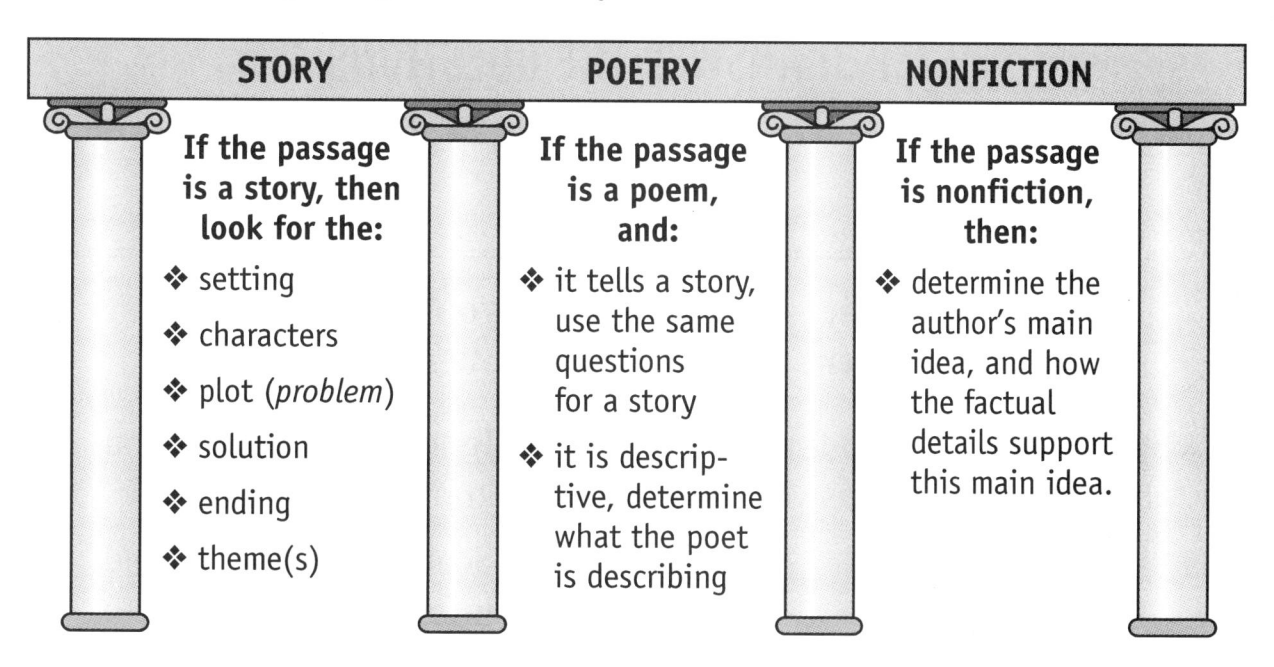

STORY	POETRY	NONFICTION
If the passage is a story, then look for the: ❖ setting ❖ characters ❖ plot (*problem*) ❖ solution ❖ ending ❖ theme(s)	If the passage is a poem, and: ❖ it tells a story, use the same questions for a story ❖ it is descriptive, determine what the poet is describing	If the passage is nonfiction, then: ❖ determine the author's main idea, and how the factual details support this main idea.

For any type of reading, you should mark key parts of the passage as you read. Marking the passage helps you to identify and recall the main details of the story. Some approaches you might want to use include:

★ (Circle) main ideas.

★ Underline key words or names that may help you follow the story, such as main characters, important conflicts, or the setting. Use a pen to mark the text.

★ Star ✱ any words or phrases that may later help you answer questions being asked. For example, identify words that show sequence or cause and effect: *as a result of, before, last, after,* etc.

★ Write comments in the margin alongside the passage. For example, write the names of characters where they first appear, or identify important events.

No one technique is right for everyone. You should experiment with these different techniques in the practice exercises in this book to see what works best for you.

STEP 3: ANSWER THE QUESTIONS

Once you have read the passage, you should begin answering the questions. For each question:

If you know the best answer, then:

Select which of the three choices you think answers the question best.

If you are not sure of the best answer, then:

→ Ignore any answers you know are not correct.

→ Scan the reading to find information relating to the question.

→ For detail, sequence, and explanation questions, look for the answer where it is directly stated in the passage.

→ If the answer is not stated, use passage details as clues to figure out the correct answer.

CHAPTER 5

ANSWERING OPEN-ENDED QUESTIONS

In the **Fourth Grade 4 Proficiency Test in Reading,** each reading selection will have one or more *open-ended questions*. Unlike a multiple-choice question which asks you to select the best choice from three possible answers, an **open-ended question** requires you to write one or more sentences of your own to answer the question. Because there are so many possibilities for your answer, these questions are called "open-ended." They are of two types:

SHORT-ANSWER QUESTIONS

Short answer questions generally focus on the details of a reading selection. They require an answer consisting of a few words or phrases, or a single sentence. Each short-answer question is worth two points. The short-answer question will only have a few lines for you to complete.

EXTENDED-RESPONSE QUESTIONS

Extended-response questions generally focus on the entire selection. These questions require an answer of several sentences. Each extended-response answer is worth four points. An extended-response answer requires that you write a more thoughtful, in-depth answer. The extended-response question will have several lines so that you can write down more ideas for your answer.

QUESTIONS THAT FOCUS ON OVERALL MEANING

Some extended-response questions will focus on your understanding of the overall meaning of a story, poem, or nonfiction passage. These questions may ask you to briefly summarize or retell the story in your own words.

SUMMARIZING A STORY

To *summarize* a story or other reading selection means to restate the topic by identifying the main idea. You are expected to write a statement in your own words reflecting the entire content of the text. Stating the main idea of a reading in one or two sentences is an important basic skill in reading that shows you fully understand what you have read. When you summarize, you should leave specific details out. Remember, the summary is shorter than the original — it "sums up" the reading in only a few sentences.

HINTS FOR ANSWERING A SUMMARIZE QUESTION

When you **summarize** a story or poem, you should include three items:

★ Describe what the story is all about.

★ State the problem faced by the characters.

★ Tell how the story ends.

★ State the theme or lesson of the story if it has one.

When you **summarize** a nonfiction selection, you should:

★ Give the main idea. Include its importance or significance.

Let's look at a sample question to see how these hints apply:

Summarize the fable of The Hare and the Tortoise.

[Describe what the story is all about]   [State the problem]

Model Answer: *The fable is about a tortoise who challenges a hare to a race. The problem faced by the tortoise is that he is much slower than the hare. Although slower, the tortoise wins the race because he goes steadily to the finish, while the arrogant hare has taken a nap. The fable shows that sometimes being slow but steady is best.*

[State the theme or lesson of the story]   [Tell how the story ends]

RETELLING A STORY

To *retell* a story or other selection is to tell it again in your own words. It helps to pretend you are telling the story to someone who has never heard it before. Be sure to have a beginning, middle and end, and to use your own words. You will not get credit for simply copying sentences from the story. Remember, a retelling is **not** a summary and can be as long as the original story. Unlike a summary, you should include important details when retelling a story, or poem, or nonfiction passage. However, do not include information not found in the original reading.

HINTS FOR ANSWERING A RETELLING QUESTION

When you **retell** *a story or poem, include the following items:*
- ★ Tell what the story is mainly about.
- ★ Introduce the main characters, and setting.
- ★ State the problem facing the characters.
- ★ Describe what happens as the story unfolds (as in a sequence map) and how it ends.

When you **retell** *a nonfiction passage, you should:*
- ★ Give the main idea and most important supporting details.
- ★ Use the same sequence in presenting details as the author did.

Let's look at a sample question to see how these hints apply:

Retell the fable of The Tortoise and the Hare.

[Tell what the story is mainly about.] [Introduce the main characters]

Model Answer: ***The Hare and the Tortoise*** *is a fable about a hare who one day makes fun of a tortoise for being slow. The tortoise then challenges the hare to a race. The hare agrees, and they appoint a fox to act as judge. When the race begins, the hare runs quickly ahead. He gets so far ahead that he decides to take a nap, showing the tortoise how foolish it was to challenge him. The tortoise keeps going, slowly and steadily. Eventually, the tortoise passes the napping hare. When the hare later awakes, it is too late for him to win the race.*

[State the problems facing the characters] [Describe what happens as the story unfolds] [Describe how the story ends]

QUESTIONS THAT FOCUS ON SPECIFIC DETAILS

Open-ended questions that focus on the specific details of a reading selection will ask you about the **what, why,** and **how** of the story, poem or nonfiction passage. They require you to examine the passage more closely or to extend its meaning.

WHAT QUESTIONS

There are actually two kinds of *what questions*. Some *what questions* ask you to explain the meaning of something. Other *what questions* ask you to explain a specific detail in the reading passage. Sometimes the question word *what* will be linked to the word *explain*.

EXPLAIN WHAT SOMETHING MEANS

This type of question asks you to explain the meaning of a statement or quotation from the story. This question tests your ability to understand the story by requiring you to explain part of the story in your own words.

Let's look at the following example based on the fable, *The Hare and the Tortoise,* which you read on page 16:

> *Explain what* this quotation from the fable *means:*
> "Slow and steady wins the race."

Model Answer: *This quotation from the fable means that people who make a constant effort often succeed, even though they may not be the fastest or the best.*

HINTS FOR ANSWERING THIS TYPE OF QUESTION

★ Use words from the question to help form your answer.

★ Think about what the statement means in the story. Then put its meaning into your own words.

★ Think of similar, more familiar words to substitute for words in the quotation.

★ Start your answer by *echoing* the question:

"The meaning of _____ is …" or "This quotation means …"

PRACTICING WHAT YOU HAVE LEARNED

Now you try. *Explain what* this quotation from the fable means: "Being over-confident may lead to failure."

This quotation from the fable means that _____

_____

_____

_____

_____

EXPLAINING SPECIFIC DETAILS

What questions can also ask you to identify or explain specific things in a reading passage. For example, this type of question might ask you to name one or more people, places, or things. Or the question might give you a general statement from the story and ask you to use specific story details to explain it. *What questions* about details may be phrased in different ways:

What did the hare do once he was far ahead in the race?

— *or* —

Explain what the hare did when he was far ahead in the race.

Model Answer: *The hare, knowing he was very far ahead in the race, took a nap.*

HINTS FOR ANSWERING THIS TYPE OF QUESTION

★ Again, start your answer by *echoing* or *repeating* the question.

★ Think about the story and look at your notes before answering.

PRACTICING WHAT YOU HAVE LEARNED

Now you try. *What* was the role of the fox in *The Hare and the Tortoise?*

The role of the fox in the story was _____

_____

_____

_____

HOW QUESTIONS

How simply means "in what way." A *how question* might ask you to explain the way in which someone changed from the beginning to the end of the story, or the way in which something in the story came about. You might read about a problem and be asked how a character solved it.

Sometimes, a *how question* may ask how a story teaches a particular lesson. A *how question* about a poem might ask you how the poem makes you feel. *How questions* might also ask how different parts of something are connected together or how something works. Here is an example of a *how question*:

Explain how the tortoise beat the hare in the race.

Model Answer: *The tortoise beat the hare in the race by always moving. The hare, once he was far ahead, stopped to take a nap. Even though the tortoise was slower than the hare, he was able to beat the hare to the finish line. The tortoise's constant effort allowed him to overcome his slow speed.*

HINTS FOR ANSWERING THIS TYPE OF QUESTION

★ The question word *how* often implies that there is a series of actions or events. In this case, your task is to show the ways in which these actions or events are connected.

★ Describe each separate event or part and show the way in which they fit together to explain the whole.

★ To *show how* a character changes, describe that character at the start of the story. Then describe each step as the character changes.

★ To tell *how* a poem makes you feel, identify the theme, images, and sounds of the poem and describe your reactions.

PRACTICING WHAT YOU HAVE LEARNED

Now you try. *How* did the tortoise respond when the hare made fun of him?

The tortoise responded when the hare made fun of him by _____

_____

_____

_____

_____

(You're so slow. How do you ever get anywhere?)

WHY QUESTIONS

Why questions generally focus on causes. To explain *why* means to give one or more reasons why something took place. Often this type of question asks you to tell about the motives or reasons that led a character to do something, or you might be asked to explain *why* something is important. Let's look at a sample question:

Explain why the hare lost the race.

Model Answer: *The hare lost the race because he was over-confident. In taking a nap, the hare lost too much time. By the time the hare woke up, the tortoise was approaching the finish line.*

HINTS FOR ANSWERING THIS TYPE OF QUESTION

★ Think about outside forces that may have caused the action or event to take place.

★ If the question asks why a character did something, think about the reasons that led the character to take that action.

★ To explain *why* something is important, think about its effects.

PRACTICING WHAT YOU HAVE LEARNED

Now you try. *Why* did the hare decide to take a nap?

The hare decided to take a nap because _____
_____
_____
_____

COMPLETING GRAPHIC ORGANIZERS

Some *open-ended questions* may ask you to complete graphic organizers. These may test your understanding of either the overall meaning or specific details. Let's examine the three most common types.

THE VENN DIAGRAM

As you learned in Chapter 1, a Venn diagram consists of two overlapping ovals (*or other shapes*) showing what two things have in common and do not have in common. It is often used to compare or contrast two situations or characters in a reading. Again, using the fable of *The Hare and the Tortoise,* answer the following sample question.

Fill in the diagram with the number next to the word that describes the hare, the number of the word that describes the tortoise, and the number of the word that describes them both. Use each number only once. Choose from:

1. over-confident
2. unafraid
3. mysterious
4. active

Hare | BOTH | Tortoise

In this type question you must fill in the blanks to complete the organizer. In the fable, the hare mocked the tortoise for being slow.

★ The tortoise was **unafraid** of racing the faster hare, because he states, "… I'll get there sooner than you think."

★ The hare was **over-confident,** since he napped during the race.

★ Both the tortoise and hare are **active,** since they participate in a race.

★ The word **mysterious** is not used, since it does not apply to any characteristic of the hare or the tortoise.

A TWO-COLUMN CHART

Another way to compare and contrast two elements in a selection is with a two-column chart. The main difference between a two-column chart and a Venn diagram is that a two-column chart has no overlapping areas. A two-column chart can be used in several different ways: (1) it could just show differences; (2) it could show similarities by listing common elements as well as differences in both columns; or (3) one column could show similarities of the two elements and the second column could list differences.

Again, let's use the fable of *The Hare and the Tortoise* to complete the following graphic.

How did the hare and the tortoise **differ**? Fill in the chart to show their **differences.**

The HARE	The TORTOISE

In the chart above, you must write a few words or phrases to describe each character. For example, the hare believed he was fast, and made fun of the hare by mocking him. Thus, for the hare you might write: *fast* and *mocked or made fun of others*. The tortoise was not afraid to accept the challenge, even though he knew he was slower. Thus, for the tortoise you could write: *accepted challenges* and *unafraid*.

THE WHEEL GRAPHIC

A wheel graphic is a form of a topic or subject map, which you learned about in Chapter 1. It is used when you want to distinguish between main ideas and supporting details in an informational passage. Look back at the selection about the Civil War on page 30 to complete the following organizer.

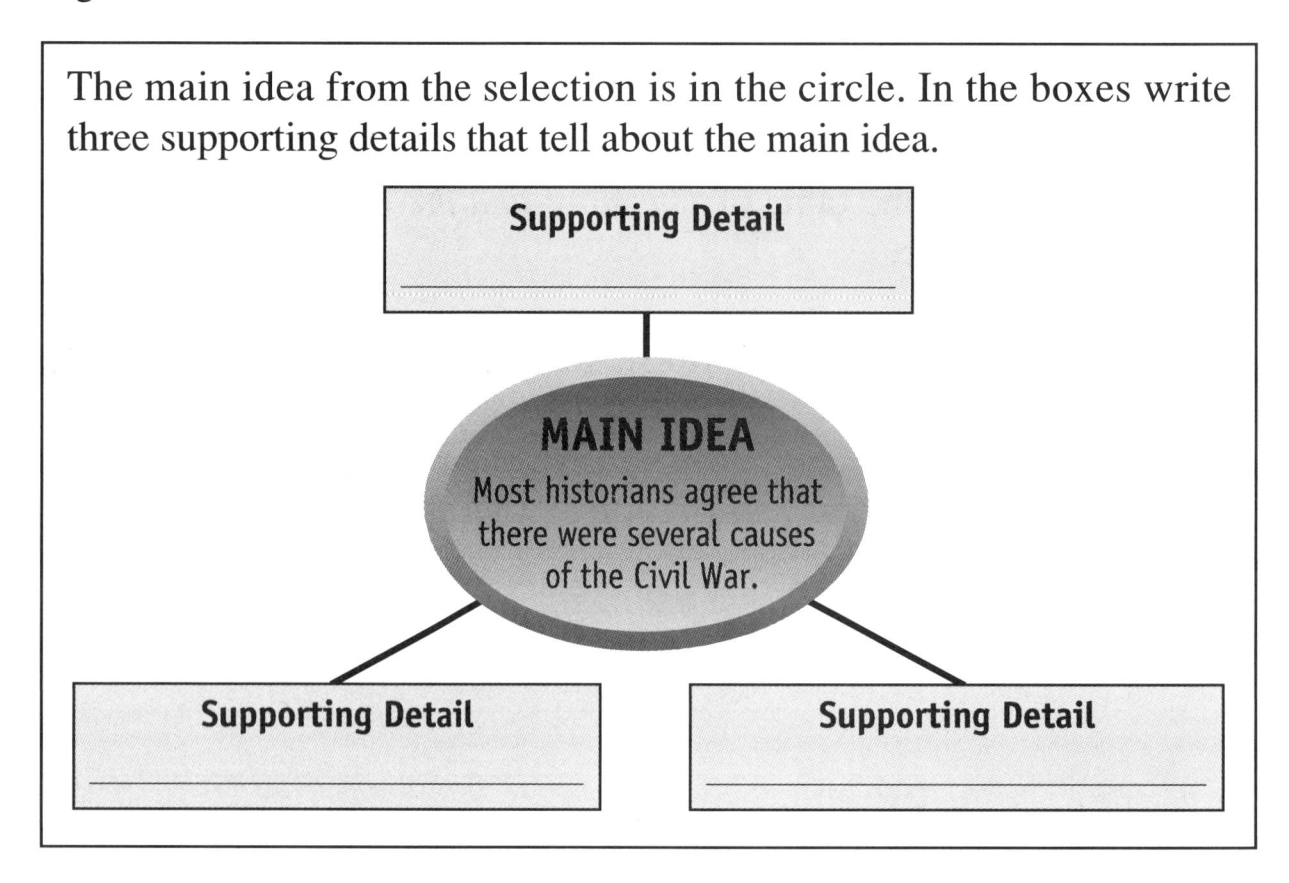

The main idea from the selection is in the circle. In the boxes write three supporting details that tell about the main idea.

Supporting Detail
_____

MAIN IDEA
Most historians agree that there were several causes of the Civil War.

Supporting Detail
_____

Supporting Detail
_____

In the wheel graphic above, you first determine what the entire reading selection is about. In this case, the opening sentence states the main idea: "Most historians agree that there were several causes of the Civil War." You next should look for details that support the main idea.

After reading the article, you can see that three separate causes are identified to show that the Civil War had more than one cause:

(1) Slavery.

(2) Concern about the spread of slavery to new states.

(3) Disagreement over states' rights.

Practice Exercises

Read the following ancient Mexican folktale called *The Poor Boy and the Emperor*. Then answer the questions about this story.

THE POOR BOY AND THE EMPEROR

Once there was an emperor who liked to disguise himself when traveling among his people, in order to learn their true opinions. One day, the emperor dressed in disguise and went into the countryside. During his wanderings, he came upon a poor young boy gathering twigs for his family.

"You hardly have enough twigs to build a fire," the emperor told the boy. "Why not collect more twigs from the royal forest across the road?"

The boy spoke to the stranger. "Kind traveler, you are not from these parts. If you were, you would know the forest belongs to the emperor. It is forbidden for anyone to enter the royal forest."

"Surely," the emperor replied, "no one would know if you went there. Your emperor must be cruel to allow twigs to lie in the forest while his subjects go cold without a fire."

continued

"I agree with you that the law is unjust," the boy said, "but the law is the law." He then walked away carrying his twigs.

Two days later the young boy and his family were summoned to the emperor's palace. When they arrived, they were brought before the emperor. The boy shuddered when he recognized that the traveler he had met was actually the emperor! He feared the emperor would punish him for speaking out against the emperor's law.

"Fear not," said the emperor. "You've done nothing wrong. You refused to steal when you had the chance, and you insisted on obeying your emperor's law. I just wanted to meet the parents who raised such an honest child."

Just then, a servant brought in a chest filled with gold, which the emperor gave to the family.

The emperor continued: "I have decided to change my law governing the royal forest. You were right. The law is unjust. From now on, all my subjects can use the forest. Your honesty has touched my heart."

Chapter 5: Answering Open-Ended Questions

1 Explain what the following two quotations from the story mean.

Quotation	Meaning
"I agree with you that the law is unjust, but the law is the law."	
"Your honesty has touched my heart."	

2 How did the young boy and the emperor each show that he was an honorable and honest person? Fill in the chart below to complete your answer.

The YOUNG BOY	The EMPEROR

3 Retell this story in detail in your own words.

CHAPTER 6

CHECKING YOUR UNDERSTANDING

Now that you have learned what will be on the **Fourth Grade Proficiency Test in Reading,** let's see how ready you are for this test.

The following pages have a group of practice readings similar to what you might expect to find on the actual test. Each passage is followed by multiple-choice and open-ended questions asking about what you have read.

You will have **35 minutes** to complete this section. Try to time yourself. This will help you get an idea of how long it takes you to complete a group of passages and questions similar to what you will find on the real test.

Directions: Read the selection and answer the questions.

Horses use sound to communicate messages to one another. Their most familiar sound is the whinny, or neigh. Whinnies can be heard half a mile away. Horses use them for communication. Each horse has its own distinctive neigh, which its friends and family can recognize. If a horse is separated from its companions, it may whinny to find where they are. An answering neigh gives their location.

When a wild horse detects danger, it snorts a warning to members of its band. A snort from a band member will bring all heads up from grazing. The animals will look in the same direction, ready to flee.

The ears of a horse are a good indicator of its mood. When a horse is dozing, its ears flop to the sides with their openings downward. If a horse that isn't sleeping holds its ears this way, it may be very tired or ill. A horse often droops its ears as a sign of giving in to another horse that is trying to dominate it. When a horse is feeling aggressive, it lays its ears flat against its head. When a horse lays its ears back, don't reach out toward its head — it might bite.

While horses' faces aren't as expressive as people's, you can still tell a great deal about how a horse is feeling from its mouth and eyes. Frightened or aggressive horses may raise their heads up and roll their eyes so that the white part shows. Pulled-back lips that reveal teeth mean they're threatening to bite. But if a young horse pulls back its lips and brings its teeth together, it's being submissive.

The tail can also reveal quite a bit about an animal's mood. Most often, the tail hangs down in a relaxed way or is used to swish away insects. But if a horse is tense or angry, it elevates the base of the tail so it sticks out away from the body. If the horse begins to flick its tail back and forth, it may be ready to kick. A horse turning its rump toward you may also be warning of a potential kick.

by Dorothy Hinshaw Patent

1. **Which sentence best tells about this article?**
   - ○ A Horses use many different methods to communicate.
   - ○ B Horses and humans can talk to each other.
   - ○ C Horses often display aggressive feelings.

2. **According to the selection, which sentence best describes why a horse might snort?**
   - ○ A When a horse faces a threat, it snorts to warn other horses.
   - ○ B A snort lets other horses know a horse is very tired.
   - ○ C Horses usually snort just before they bite someone.

3. **If a horse's ears flop to the side and the ear's openings point down, what would you expect the horse to be doing?**
   - ○ A Eating
   - ○ B Sleeping
   - ○ C Kicking

4. **Which sentence best explains why horses snort, whinny, or neigh?**
   - ○ A These sounds are used as forms of communication.
   - ○ B These sounds indicate that a horse is happy and content.
   - ○ C These sounds are used to alert other horses of a pending attack.

5. **Why might two horses from the same group neigh to one another?**
   - ○ A They are preparing to run away.
   - ○ B They are trying to locate each other.
   - ○ C They are getting ready to attack each other.

6. **Which of the following would be a good book to use if you wanted to find out more about the topic of this selection?**
   - ○ A *How to Raise Horses*
   - ○ B *America's Greatest Race Horses*
   - ○ C *The Animals of North America*

7 **What do ear and tail movements tell you about a horse's mood? Fill in the chart below to complete your answer.**

EAR MOVEMENTS	TAIL MOVEMENTS

8 **If you were a horse, explain some of the ways you might communicate your feelings. Use information from the article to answer this question.**

Directions: Read the poem and answer the questions.

CITY, CITY
by Marci Ridlon

I
City, city
Wrong and bad,
Looms above me
When I'm sad,
Throws its shadow
On my care,
Sheds its poison
In my air,
Pounds me with its
Noisy fist,
Sprays me with its
Sooty mist.
Till, with sadness
On my face,
I long to live
Another place.

II
City, city,
Golden-clad,
Shines around me
When I'm glad,
Lifts me with its
Strength and height,
Fills me with its
Sound and sight,
Takes me to its
Crowded heart,
Holds me so I
Won't depart.
Till, with gladness
On my face,
I wouldn't live
Another place.

9 Which sentence best summarizes this poem?
- A The poet has mixed feelings about city living.
- B Many things cause pollution in the city.
- C The poet is going to move to the countryside.

10 What does the poet mean when she says the city "Sheds its poison in my air"?
- A Someone is trying to kill people living in the city.
- B The city is a place filled with pollution.
- C There are dangerous animals in the city spitting out poison.

11 Which phrase would best fit in box 1?
- A bright sunshine
- B sooty mist
- C deep loneliness

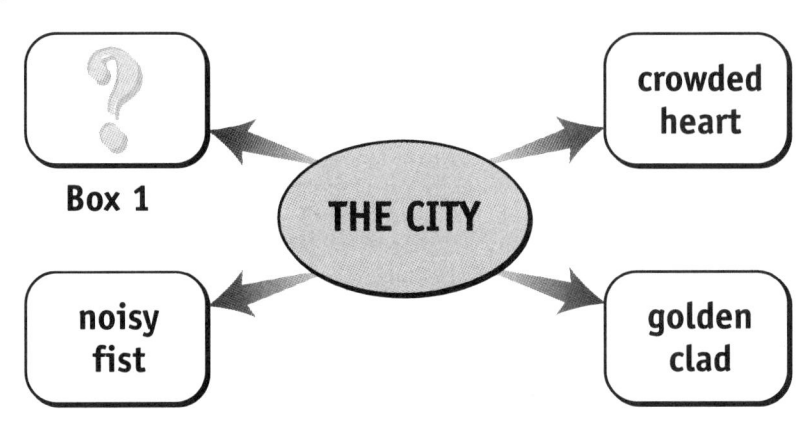

```
                                              crowded
      ?                                        heart
    Box 1        THE CITY
    noisy                                     golden
    fist                                       clad
```

12 Which statement best expresses the poet's feelings?
- A The poet hates city living when she is sad, but finds strength in the city when she is happy.
- B The poet hopes to leave the city because of its noise, dirt, and pollution.
- C The city fills the poet with strength, especially when she is sad.

13 Use information from the poem to tell how the city makes the poet feel when she is glad.

_____

_____

_____

_____

_____

Directions: Read the selection and answer the questions.

The folktale below comes from ancient China. It explores the relationship between a mother and her child.

There once was a young man named Li who devoted himself to the task of taking care of his old widowed mother. He cooked for her, made sure she took her medicine every night, and brought old friends to see her so that she wouldn't be lonely. And once a week, he took her to his father's resting place where she grieved quietly while Li swept away the dirt from the grave.

One evening a thief broke into their house. He made Li and the old woman sit in the corner while he searched the place. He carried a cloth bag and began stuffing it with whatever he thought worth stealing.

He took Li's silk robe, the only piece of good clothing the youth possessed. Li watched and said nothing. He took Li's jacket, the only one he had to keep warm on bitter cold mornings. The youth again kept silent. He took Li's jade ring, which Li's father had given to him. The young man's lip trembled, but still he said nothing.

Then the thief reached for an old pot. "Please, be kind enough to leave us that old pot," Li spoke up. "If you take it, I won't be able to make my mother's dinner."

The thief dropped the pot and looked in awe at the young man and his mother. "Heaven will surely curse me if I rob a house where such duty lives," he cried. He emptied his bag and left with a softened heart.

14 What would be the best title for this story?
  ○ **A** One Boy's Sense of Responsibility
  ○ **B** Li Visits His Father's Resting Place
  ○ **C** Growing Old in China

15 What lesson does the thief learn from Li?
  ○ **A** Crime does not pay.
  ○ **B** Loyalty to a parent is more important than material objects.
  ○ **C** Never fear someone who is trying to steal your property.

16 Why does the thief empty his bag and leave?
  ○ **A** He is afraid of being caught by the police.
  ○ **B** He is impressed by the young boy's loyalty to his mother.
  ○ **C** He wants to save himself before he is caught stealing.

17 Why does Li bring old friends to visit with his mother?
  ○ **A** He is friendly with his mother's friends.
  ○ **B** He does not want his mother to be lonely.
  ○ **C** He likes to be around older people.

18 Read the numbered words below. Fill in the diagram with the number of a word to describe Li, the number of a word to describe the thief, and the number of a word to describe them both. Use each numbered word only once. Choose from:
  1. loyal
  2. dishonest
  3. caring
  4. unforgiving

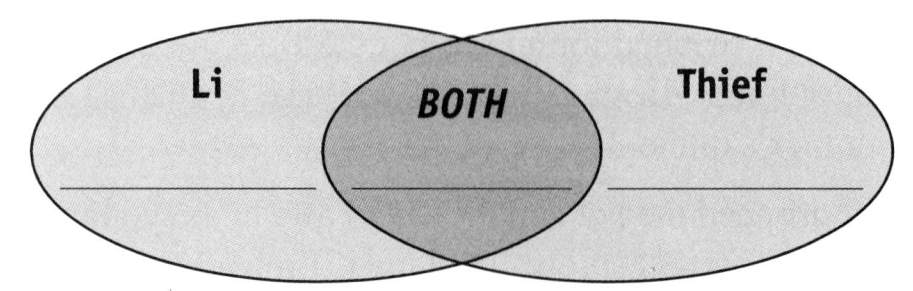

19 **What word would best fit in Box 1?**
- A devoted
- B sickly
- C lazy

Box 1 ← LI → young
son ← LI → patient

20 **The story mentions the only good piece of clothing that Li *possessed*. What does *possessed* mean?**
- A spooky
- B needed
- C owned

21 **The folktale says that the thief "looked in awe" at Li. What does *looked in awe* mean?**
- A was frightened by Li
- B showed hatred on his face
- C looked with wonder and surprise

22 **Retell the story in detail.**

Directions: Read the story and answer the questions.

An Old Man's Advice

A father who had grown tired from frequent failures in life decided to visit a famous wise old man. "Help me," he cried. "I'm so tired of failing. At least half the time, whatever I do does not seem to work out. What should I do?"

"I'll tell you what to do," said the wise old man. "Look on page 720 of the *World Almanac*. There you will find the answer to dealing with life's problems."

The father hurried off to the library. He was excited at the possibility of discovering such an important secret. He rushed to where the *World Almanac* could be found. He quickly turned to the right page, and found a list of the lifetime batting averages of the greatest baseball players. At the top of the list stood the name Ty Cobb, the most successful baseball hitter of all time. His average was .367.

The bewildered father returned to see the wise man. "I don't understand," he said. "What does Ty Cobb's batting average have to do with finding the answer to dealing with my failures in life?"

"Ty Cobb's average was .367," the wise old man replied. "One out of every three times he stood at the plate, he got a hit. But two out of every three times, he failed to get a hit. And yet he was the greatest!"

23 Which sentence best tells about this selection?
- A Ty Cobb's reputation as a baseball player was poor.
- B People must learn how to deal with failure.
- C Most important information can be found in an almanac.

24 Why does the father visit the famous wise old man?
- A to borrow some money
- B to seek advice about his life
- C to hear a story about Ty Cobb

25 How often did Ty Cobb get a hit when he played baseball?
- A almost every time he batted
- B about half the time
- C once every three times at bat

26 If the wise old man were to say another sentence at the end of the story, what would it be?
- A "Don't be discouraged by failure, keep trying."
- B "We should learn never to listen to the advice of old men."
- C "So you see, Ty Cobb was not really a great ball player."

27 In this story, the bewildered father returns to see the wise man. What does *bewildered* mean?
- A angry
- B puzzled
- C educated

28 Who is telling this story?
- A Ty Cobb
- B A wise old man
- C A narrator

29 **Which of the following would be a good book to use if you wanted to learn what kind of person Ty Cobb was?**
- A *How to Play Baseball*
- B *Baseball's Greatest Players*
- C *The World Almanac*

30 Summarize the story.

UNIT 2: WRITING

- **Chapter 7:** The Elements of Good Writing
- **Chapter 8:** Writing a Fictional Narrative
- **Chapter 9:** Writing about Your Personal Experiences
- **Chapter 10:** Writing a Report
- **Chapter 11:** Writing Letters, Journals, and Directions
- **Chapter 12:** Checking Your Understanding

This part of the book focuses on preparing you for the **Fourth Grade Proficiency Test in Writing.** The test will require you to write a long essay and a shorter piece. Writing under pressure can be difficult as well as frustrating. This unit will help you to prepare for the writing test by giving you practice with different kinds of writing. If you carefully review the skills in this unit, you should be able to complete an interesting and well-written essay on the test.

CHAPTER 7

THE ELEMENTS OF GOOD WRITING

The **Fourth Grade Proficiency Test in Writing** will require you to provide two writing samples. First you will be given a writing "topic" or "prompt." A **prompt** is something that makes people think and causes them to respond. The prompt might be a short story or article that you read along with your teacher, who reads it aloud. The prompt might also be a picture, or an idea or scene described by your teacher.

After you look over and study the prompt, you will be asked to complete a pre-writing exercise. This exercise will not be scored, but will help you to develop ideas for your two writing samples. Even though you will not get a score for the pre-writing exercise, you should take this exercise very seriously. It will serve as a springboard for many of the ideas you will later develop in your writing samples. Take your time in completing it. Do not go ahead and look at the test questions that follow. Instead, try to focus on the pre-writing exercise and developing several good ideas.

In completing the pre-writing exercise, jot down your ideas in note form without using full sentences. For example, you may read a story about what will happen in the future. For the pre-writing exercise, you could be asked to jot down what you think will happen in the future, and also what you think will not happen. As a second example, you might be asked to read an article in order to write a report. In the pre-writing exercise, you could be asked to fill out note cards for your report.

After you complete the pre-writing exercise, you will be given directions for completing the two writing assignments, which will be scored. Each assignment will require a different kind of writing.

Usually, you will have to write a long piece (identified as **Exercise A**) and a short piece (identified as **Exercise B**). Some of the types of writing you may be required to complete are the following:

EXAMPLES OF *EXERCISE A* WRITING

★ **An Fictional Narrative.** This is a story you make up that is not true, but based on some topic or theme related to the test stimulus.

★ **A Personal Experience Essay.** This is an essay based on your own personal experiences. It may be true or it may include some details that are not true.

★ **A Report.** This is a nonfiction writing based on information in the test prompt, in which you provide a description or explanation to your reader.

EXAMPLES OF *EXERCISE B* WRITING

★ **A Communication.** You may be asked to write some type of communication, such as a friendly letter, invitation, thank-you note, letter to the editor, directions, or journal entry.

The rest of this chapter will give you some general guidance on how to write and organize your answers for **Ohio's Fourth Grade Proficiency Test in Writing.** Later chapters will provide you with practice in the specific types of writing you may be asked to complete on the test.

THE CHARACTERISTICS OF GOOD WRITING

What makes a good writer? Whatever type of writing you are asked to complete, your work should have the following four characteristics:

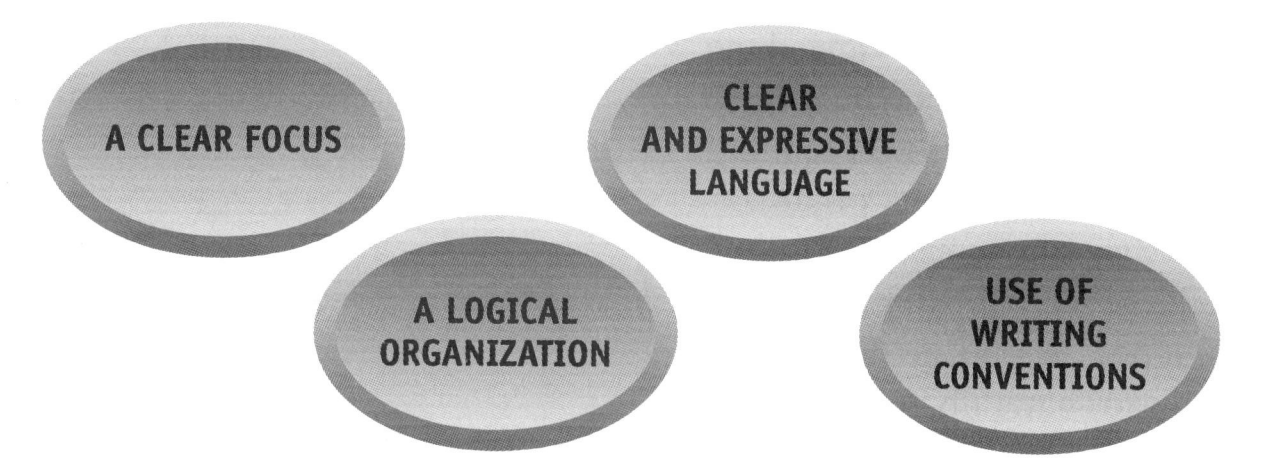

- A CLEAR FOCUS
- CLEAR AND EXPRESSIVE LANGUAGE
- A LOGICAL ORGANIZATION
- USE OF WRITING CONVENTIONS

A CLEAR FOCUS

You need to have a clear focus in your writing to communicate your ideas effectively. A clear focus begins by identifying the topic you are writing about somewhere near the beginning of your essay. Everything else you write should relate in some way to that topic. Think of your topic as an umbrella that covers the rest of your essay, report, story or letter. It provides a unifying theme that brings the different parts of your writing together into a unified whole.

On the **Fourth Grade Proficiency Test in Writing,** the requirements of the question will determine your focus. First, read the prompt carefully. Then, complete the pre-writing exercise. Finally, read the directions to each writing assignment carefully. Study the **words** in the question so that you clearly understand what you are supposed to do. Then keep your writing focused on those requirements. In order to keep your writing focused, it is important to plan your answers before you write.

A LOGICAL ORGANIZATION

Organization refers to the order in which you present your ideas to the reader. Your writing should not ramble from one thought to another. It must be logical enough to permit the reader to follow what you have written about without becoming confused.

After you have reviewed the directions, plan your answer to have a logical flow. Planning is essential to good organization. Make sure your ideas follow one another logically. A logical sequence is one in which one idea leads naturally to the next.

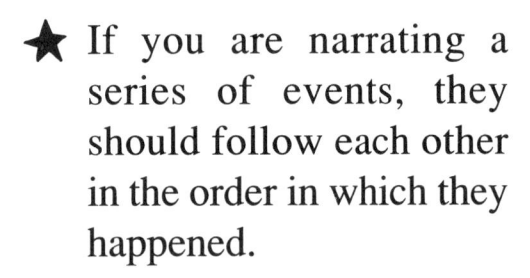

★ If you are narrating a series of events, they should follow each other in the order in which they happened.

★ If you are writing a report, each of your main ideas or subtopics should be followed by supporting details. Think of the best order for presenting your main ideas. You might proceed from specific examples to a general conclusion, or present several general statements, going from least to most important.

★ If you are giving directions or explaining a process, divide your explanation into a series of steps. Use a separate paragraph for each step.

Think of your essay as a chain. Each part is attached to and closely linked to the preceding part and the following part. This means that each sentence in every paragraph must clearly be connected to the previous sentence. Just as sentences are connected to each other, each paragraph must also be connected to the next paragraph.

To help make your organization clearer to your reader, you must use transitions. A **transition** is a guidepost that signals to the reader that you are moving from one point to another. Some common transitional phrases are: "*moreover,*" "*for example,*" "*in conclusion,*" "*therefore,*" "*in addition,*" "*next,*" "*the following day,*" or "*another reason.*" Use these transitional phrases to introduce each main idea or event you are discussing. Here is how transitions might appear in an essay answer:

★ *Another reason* he did not go to work that day was because his car was not working."

★ *In addition,* he didn't realize they only had two weeks to complete the project.

★ *Next,* he gathered up as much money as he could find in the house.

These transitions allow your reader to logically follow what you are writing about.

CLEAR AND EXPRESSIVE LANGUAGE

To achieve clarity in your answer, you need to express yourself precisely. In writing your answer, try to use vivid language, specific details, and varied sentence patterns. Try to communicate your own enthusiasm to the reader. Also be sure to use legible handwriting, in print or cursive.

It would be boring if you used the same tone whenever you spoke. You naturally vary the tone of your voice when you speak of an exciting or interesting event. Your writing needs the same kind of variety and excitement. Sentences should be imaginative and lively. One way to make your writing interesting is to use sentences that vary in length and style. Sentences should range from the simple to the complex.

If you are supposed to write your answer from a particular point of view, then write a response showing how you think that person would feel. Use language appropriate to your particular purpose and audience.

USE OF WRITING CONVENTIONS

In writing your answers it is also important to follow the conventions of written English. Although your work on the **Fourth Grade Proficiency Test in Writing** will be scored as a first draft, you must be careful to avoid major errors in grammar, spelling, capitalization and punctuation. These include such mistakes as:

★ run-on sentences

★ a subject and verb that are not in agreement

★ missing or incorrect punctuation

★ the misspelling of common words

Remember that major errors in the conventions of written English will lower your test score.

> **NOTE:** To help you avoid making errors in the conventions of written English, you will find *A Handbook of Grammar and Writing Mechanics* in the back of this book. The *Handbook* is provided to help you review the major rules of grammar and usage that you will be responsible for in your writing.

Now that you have reviewed the essential characteristics of writing, let's look more closely at how to organize your answer.

ORGANIZING YOUR WRITTEN RESPONSE

A good written response is usually organized into three parts:

INTRODUCTION

When we first meet a stranger, it is customary to introduce ourselves. Similarly, in writing, you should begin with an introduction. The introduction is where you tell your reader what your response will be about. Your introduction may be as short as a single sentence, or it could be your entire first paragraph.

BODY

The body is the main part of your answer. The body gives your main ideas about the topic, along with their supporting details.

★ If you are writing about a significant event in your life, the body of your response should provide specific examples that recount or tell about the event.

★ If you are writing about something you observed, you will need to describe and record your reaction to the event.

CONCLUSION

When we leave someone, we say goodbye to let them know that we are going. At the end of any writing piece, you should similarly say goodbye to your reader by writing a conclusion.

In your conclusion, you may want to quickly summarize your main ideas. However, a conclusion is often more than simply a summary. You may want to state some general moral or lesson that can be learned from what you have written about.

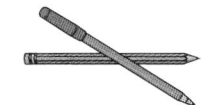

THE WRITING PROCESS

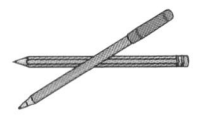

Now you are ready to examine the writing process. Writing a response on the test is usually a four-step process:

STEP 1: ANALYZE THE QUESTION

Each writing exercise has specific instructions indicating what you should do. You must examine "question" words such as *what, how,* or *why* to find out what you are supposed to do. The "question" words generally have the same meaning as they do for questions on the **Fourth Grade Proficiency Test in Reading.** See pages 3 and 4 to review the meanings of these words. After examining the "question" words, take a moment to think about what the question asks. Usually the question will ask you to make use of some of the ideas you developed in the pre-writing exercise.

STEP 2: PLAN AND PRE-WRITE

Next, make an outline of your answer in the form of a special drawing. Imagine your drawing resembles a hamburger with a top bun, patties of meat, and a bottom bun. The top bun is your introduction, the patties of meat form the body of your answer, and the bottom bun is your conclusion.

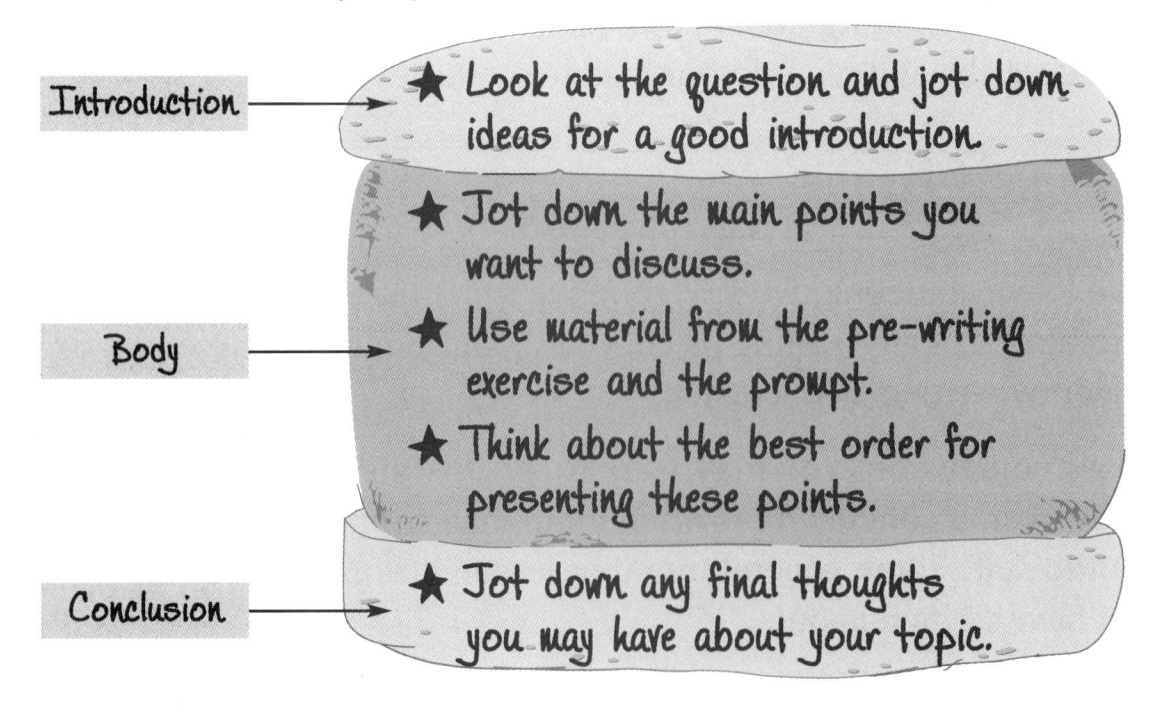

Introduction
★ Look at the question and jot down ideas for a good introduction.

Body
★ Jot down the main points you want to discuss.
★ Use material from the pre-writing exercise and the prompt.
★ Think about the best order for presenting these points.

Conclusion
★ Jot down any final thoughts you may have about your topic.

STEP 3: WRITE YOUR ANSWER

This step requires turning your hamburger (*outline*) into a finished product.

INTRODUCTION

Start with your introduction sentence *(or sentences)*. Often, your introduction will identify the topic of your written response. You now must lead your reader from the introduction to the body of your answer. Writers use transition sentences to accomplish this movement. Remember, a **transition sentence** moves a reader from one major idea to another.

BODY

Next you must write the body, or main part, of your answer. Turn each of the points of your outline into complete sentences. Make sure to cover all the points asked in the question. Try to be as descriptive and detailed as possible. For example:

★ Mention particular details if you are writing about something that happened to you personally.

★ Give interesting details in your essay. Don't forget to use direct quotations if you can recall them.

CONCLUSION

End your answer with one or more concluding sentences. Remember, conclusions are often more than summaries. The conclusion should show what resulted from the events you described, or what can be learned. Your conclusion may even make suggestions or recommendations.

STEP 4: REVISE AND EDIT

You need to read over your answer to see if you have included all your main ideas. Revise your essay to improve its organization or to add anything you left out. Re-reading also allows you to check your answer for errors. Remember that writing errors can lower your test score. This process of checking your work is sometimes called **editing.**

In this chapter, you have examined the characteristics of good writing, the writing process, and how to organize your response. In later chapters you will learn how to use these general techniques with different kinds of writing.

Keep in mind that whatever type of writing you are assigned, your response must show the following:

✔ CHECKLIST

- ☐ A response that stays on the topic
- ☐ The use of details to support the topic
- ☐ An organized and logical response that flows naturally, and has a beginning, middle, and end
- ☐ The use of a variety of words and sentence patterns
- ☐ A response that shows an awareness of word usage (vocabulary, homonyms, and words in context)
- ☐ A response that shows an awareness of spelling patterns for commonly used words
- ☐ Legible writing in print or cursive
- ☐ The correct use of capital letters (beginning of sentences and for proper nouns) and end punctuation.

Practice Exercises

> We meet many different people in our lives. Many of these people do not leave a strong impression on us. Sometimes, however, we meet someone whom we will remember for the rest of our lives. Describe someone you have met whom you know you will remember for the rest of your life.

For this question do not write out your response. Instead, practice pre-writing your response using the hamburger outline below:

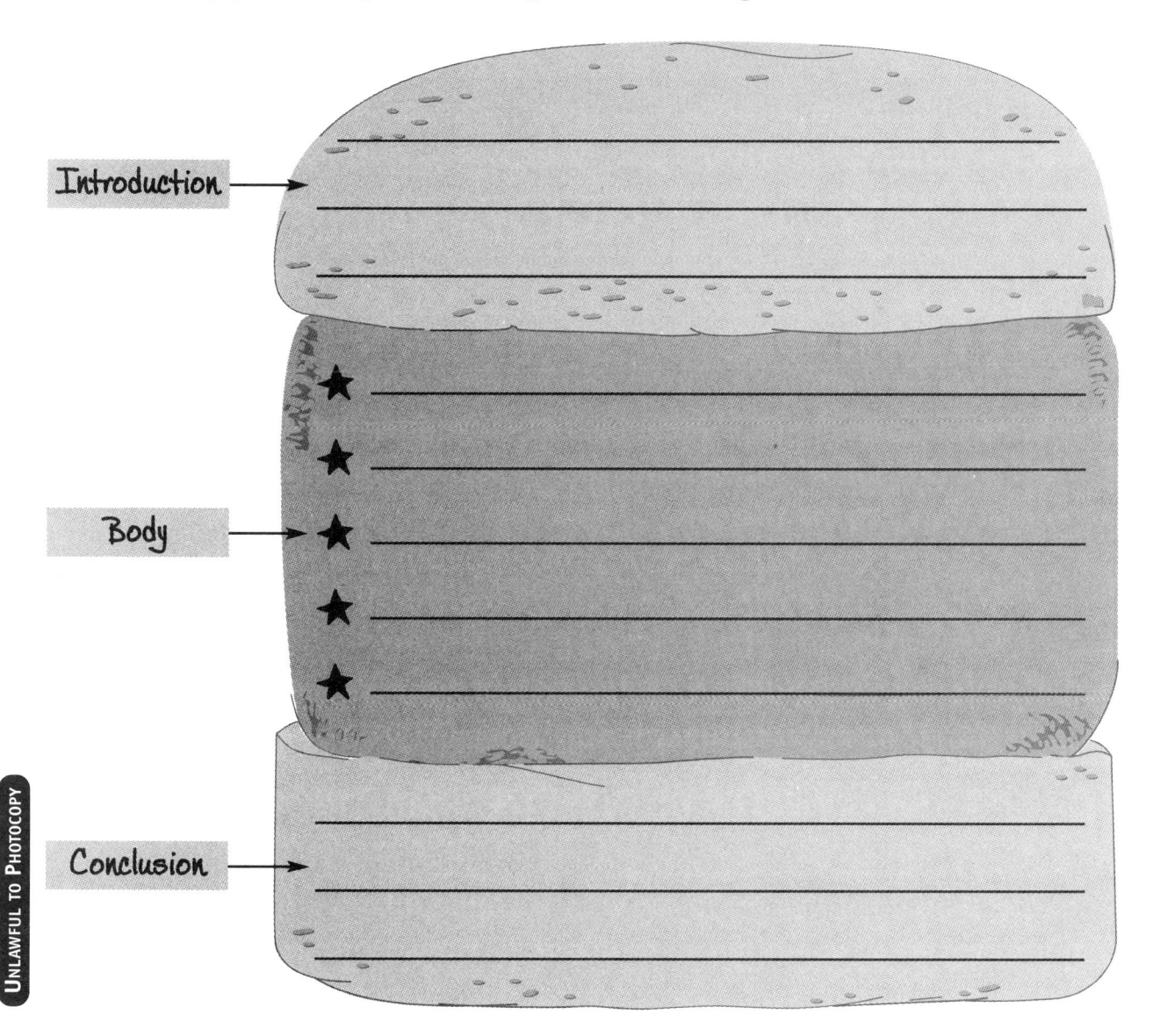

Introduction

Body
- ★
- ★
- ★
- ★
- ★

Conclusion

Our lives are often filled with both pain and joy. Sometimes, we feel happy or sad about big things — like an important achievement or a death in the family. Other times, we are moved by smaller things that affect our mood — like pretty flowers on a summer day. Write about something good or bad that gave you either pain or joy. Describe what happened and your feelings about it.

For this question again do not write out your response. Instead, practice pre-writing your response using the hamburger outline below:

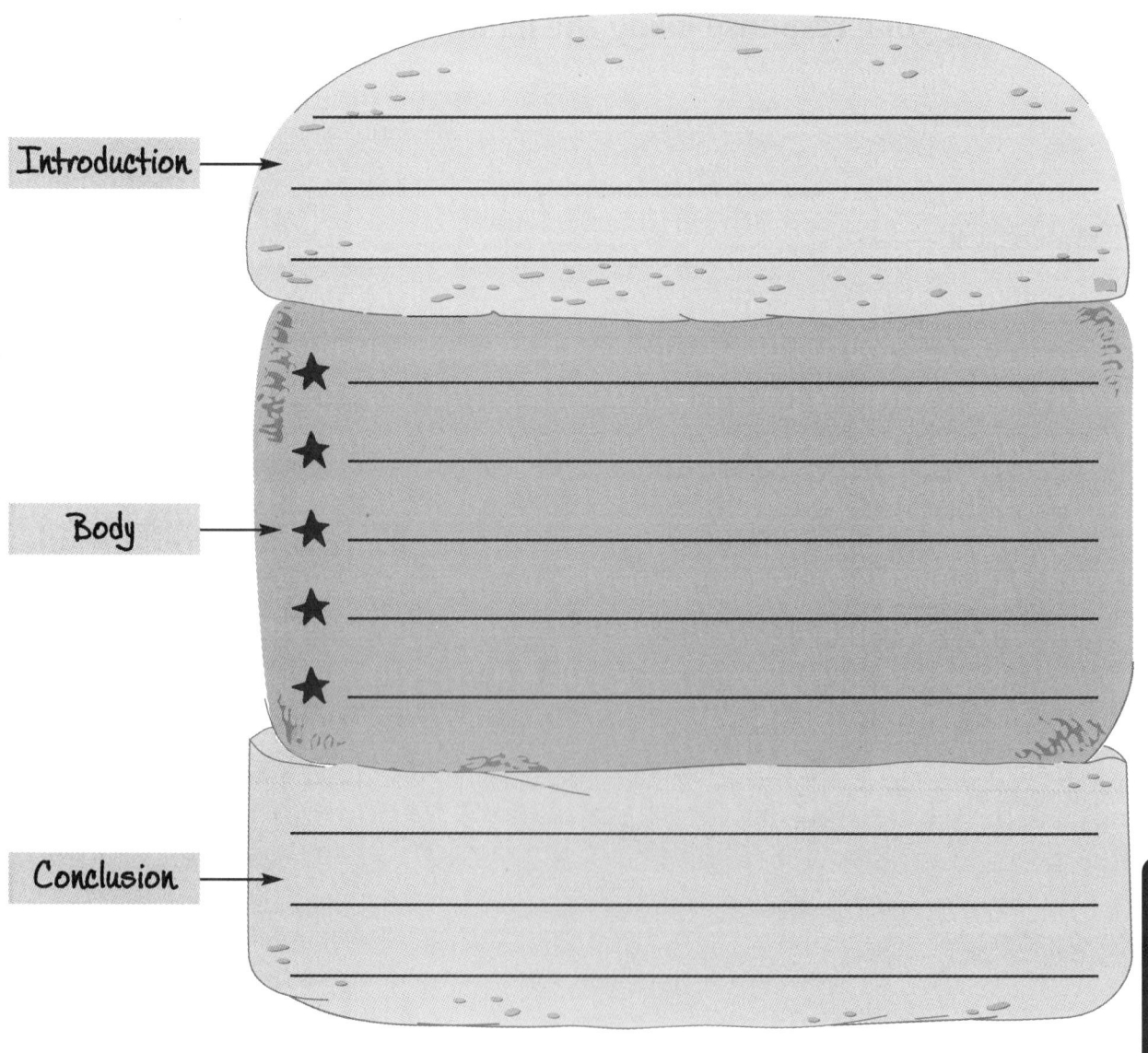

Introduction

Body
- ★
- ★
- ★
- ★
- ★

Conclusion

CHAPTER 8

WRITING A FICTIONAL NARRATIVE

One of the types of writing you may be asked to do on Exercise A of the **Fourth Grade Proficiency Test in Writing** is a fictional narrative. This type of writing requires you to tell a fictional story. **Fictional** stories are not true, but come from your imagination. A **narrative** is a story in which someone relates a series of events. The narrator could be a character in the story or an impartial story-teller.

You have read many fictional stories in school and at home. You also learned about the elements of a fictional story earlier in this book. In this chapter, you will learn how to write a fictional narrative of your own.

WRITING A FICTIONAL NARRATIVE

You may be given a topic to write about, or you may be asked to write a story based on some prompt, such as an illustration or story. In writing your own story, you will be required to establish:

- Setting
- Characters
- Plot

Your story should have a clear beginning with some interesting problem or challenge that the characters must overcome. The test directions or prompt may provide you with the problem or topic of your story.

Although there are several ways you can create an original story, we recommend that you start by focusing on the basic elements of a story — setting, characters, and plot. Then end your story with a conclusion, which may include a statement of your theme.

SETTING (*Where and when your story takes place.*)

First, your introduction should describe the setting. For example,

> Jones Elementary School was located in the town of Centerville. Although small in population, Centerville was one of the most interesting and unique places to live.

PRACTICING WHAT YOU HAVE LEARNED

Now write a sentence or two giving the **setting** to a story of your own:

CHARACTERS

Next, you should introduce the characters of your story. Since these characters come from your own imagination, you are the only one who knows what they look like. Name and describe something about each of your characters as they appear in the story. To make the story more interesting, you may even want to have the characters speak to each other in a conversation.

> Kayla, a fourth-grade student at Jones Elementary, was one of the most popular girls in her class. Kayla's father, John, was a hard-working clothes salesman.

PRACTICING WHAT YOU HAVE LEARNED

Now you should introduce one or more **characters** of your own story: _____

_____

_____

PLOT

For the plot, you need to introduce a problem. The problem sets the stage for the action of the story. Make the problem challenging and realistic. It could deal with natural obstacles, human relationships, or personal goals. For example,

> Kayla had always dreamed that her parents would buy her a new bicycle for her birthday. However, her father lost his job, and the family faced hard economic times. Would Kayla ever get the bicycle she dreamed of?

PRACTICING WHAT YOU HAVE LEARNED

Now you should introduce a **problem** that will set the stage for the action in your story: _____

_____

_____

_____

_____

_____

_____

The rest of the plot should describe a series of events that unfold when the characters in the story try to solve the problem. Be sure to include some interesting and specific details when describing these events. The characters and their goals may also change as a result of these events.

> Kayla decided to get a part-time job after school baby-sitting for her neighbor. Her mother chipped in by walking to work every day in order to save the cost of riding the bus. Soon, with the help of her family, Kayla had saved enough money to buy herself a shiny new bicycle. That spring, Kayla bought her new bicycle.

CHAPTER 8: WRITING A FICTIONAL NARRATIVE   99

PRACTICING WHAT YOU HAVE LEARNED

Next, you should give the rest of the **plot** of your story:

CONCLUSION (*Ending*)

The conclusion is the ending of your story. You might also show how this particular story illustrates a general lesson in life. For example,

> This story shows that when a family works together, it can overcome many problems.

PRACTICING WHAT YOU HAVE LEARNED

Now you should **conclude** your story:

Practice Exercises

WRITING A FICTIONAL NARRATIVE

Below is an illustration of three students riding in a school bus. They are all laughing very loudly.

PRE-WRITING

Directions: Look at the illustration of these students riding in the school bus. What is happening in the illustration? Where are the students going? What do you think they have been talking about? What could have caused them to laugh out loud? Take time to read and answer the questions that follow. The pre-writing activity will help you get the ideas for the story you will make up. The pre-writing work will not be scored.

1. **What is happening in the illustration?** Write as many details as you can think of based on the illustration. Then put a check next to each thing you noticed that you want to use in your story.

2. **What do you think the students on the bus have been talking about?** Think about what they might be saying to each other. Write as many ideas as you can think of. Then put a check by the ones that you choose for your story.

3. **What could have caused them to laugh aloud?** Were they laughing at something or someone? Who might have said something that was so funny? Write down as many reasons for their laughter as you can think of. Then put a check next to the reason you like best.

FICTIONAL NARRATIVE — Story you make up

Now you are going to make up or invent a story about the students on the school bus. The story you write will be scored. Look at the box below. It shows what your best paper must have.

☑ CHECKLIST

I will earn my best score if:

- ❑ My made-up story gives the names of the main characters.
- ❑ My made-up story tells what is happening in the illustration.
- ❑ My made-up story tells what the students are talking about.
- ❑ My made-up story tells what caused the students to laugh.
- ❑ My made-up story has a beginning, middle, and end.
- ❑ I use words that make my meaning clear. I do not use the same words over and over.
- ❑ I try to spell the words correctly.
- ❑ My sentences and proper names begin with a capital letter.
- ❑ My sentences end with a period, an exclamation mark, or a question mark.

Directions: You will make up a story about the students on the school bus. Your story will tell about what or whom they were talking about and what caused them to laugh. Look back at the pre-writing and use the things you checked for your story. Your story should make sense and have a beginning, a middle, and an end. Be sure to use words that make your meaning clear. Write your story on the following pages.

Chapter 8: Writing a Fictional Narrative

Before writing your fictional narrative, plan your response by using the hamburger outline below:

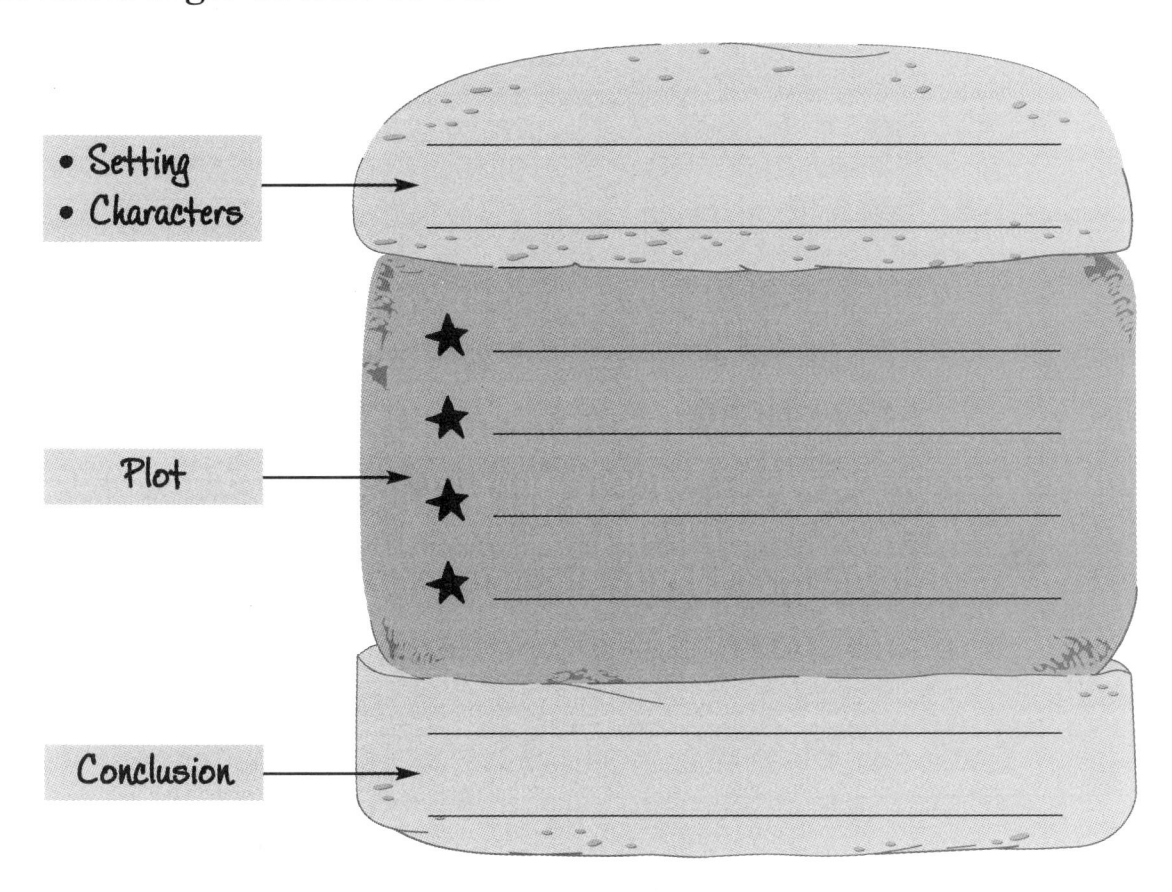

- Setting
- Characters

Plot

Conclusion

Now write your fictional narrative below:

When you finish writing your fictional narrative, use the checklist on page 102 to revise and edit your work. When you have finished checking your essay and you are satisfied with it, you are finished.

CHAPTER 9

WRITING ABOUT YOUR PERSONAL EXPERIENCES

A second type of writing found on Exercise A of **Ohio's Fourth Grade Proficiency Test in Writing** asks you to write a story or essay based on your personal experiences. In this type of writing, you must use *experiences from your life* or the life of someone you know or know about.

You may feel somewhat uncomfortable writing about yourself. Remember, testmakers are not concerned with your actual personal experiences, but with your ability to write. The directions may even tell you that your story does not have to be completely true. If you cannot remember all the details of the experience, it is acceptable to make up a few.

HOW TO WRITE ABOUT YOUR PERSONAL EXPERIENCES

Let's return to the fable, *The Hare and the Tortoise,* as a prompt for writing about your personal experiences. In that story, the tortoise, although slower than the speedy hare, won the race. One of the morals to the story was that working hard can often bring about positive results. The pre-writing exercise will help you to develop your ideas.

PRE-WRITING

Now you will do some thinking and planning for a narrative of your own, based on your personal experiences. The pre-writing exercise will help you plan your essay.

Directions: Think of a time when you found that working hard can bring positive results. Think about your own experiences. Take time to read and answer the questions that follow. The pre-writing activity will help you get ideas for your narrative.

1. **What were you working on?** Was it something you were making, writing, or designing? Was it part of a competition? Write down as many details as you can remember. Then put a check next to the most interesting ones for your story.

2. **How did you work hard?** Did you spend a lot of time on the project? Did you require great physical or mental effort? Did you continue to work when it seemed unlikely you would succeed? Write down as many details as you can think of. Then put a check next to the ones you like the best.

3. **What were the positive results you achieved?** What changes did you bring about? What benefits did you obtain or give to others? Write down as many details as you can think of. Then put a check next to the ones you like the best.

A NARRATIVE ABOUT YOUR PERSONAL EXPERIENCES

Now you are going to write about a time in your life when you learned that working hard can bring positive results. The story you write will be scored. Look at the box below. It shows what your best paper must have.

✔ CHECKLIST

I will earn my best score if:

- ☐ My personal experience essay describes what I was working on.
- ☐ My personal experience essay tells how I worked hard.
- ☐ My personal experience essay tells about the positive results I achieved.
- ☐ My personal experience essay has a beginning, middle, and end.
- ☐ I use words that make my meaning clear. I do not use the same words over and over.
- ☐ I try to spell the words correctly.
- ☐ My sentences and proper names begin with a capital letter.
- ☐ My sentences end with a period, an exclamation mark, or a question mark.

Directions: You will write a personal experience essay about a time when you found that working hard can bring positive results. Your personal experience essay will tell about the situation, how it came about, and what happened. Look back at the pre-writing page in which you answered certain questions, and use the things you checked for your personal experience essay. Your personal experience essay should make sense and have a beginning, a middle, and an end. Be sure to use words that make your meaning clear.

Based on the ideas you developed in the pre-writing exercise, you should first create an outline to answer this question.

Introduction. In the introduction, tell your reader what you will be writing about. Introduce yourself (*or someone else*) as the subject of your essay. Set the scene by giving details about the time and place.

Body. In the body, tell your reader about your experiences related to the theme of the essay. Draw on material you wrote in your pre-writing notes. Provide the reader with details about what you are writing on. You can do this by telling the *how, what, why, who,* and *where* about the theme. Make the essay interesting by focusing on a problem or challenge and how you or someone else overcame it.

Conclusion. Conclude by relating your essay to the overall theme. You might explain how your hard work finally paid off.

Now write an outline, based on the ideas in your pre-writing exercise. Although a "hamburger" outline will not appear on the test, you may wish to use it to help you plan your essay.

Introduction
★ _____
★ _____

Body
★ _____
★ _____
★ _____
★ _____

Conclusion
★ _____
★ _____

INTRODUCTION TO YOUR ESSAY

After you have completed your outline, you should begin writing your answer. Remember that a personal narrative should always be written in the "first person" — I — with you acting as the narrator.

> *People sometimes say that hard work brings positive results. No one taught me that better than my friend Matt Einstein. Matt and I were nine years old when we first became friends. He was tall and skinny, with short brown hair. What really made Matt stand out was that he had problems hearing. I had heard about people with hearing problems before, but Matt was the first such person I ever met. He had to use a hearing aid to hear what was going on in class.*

PRACTICING WHAT YOU HAVE LEARNED

Now write an introduction to your own essay about a time you learned that hard work can bring positive results. _____

_____
_____
_____
_____
_____
_____

THE BODY OF YOUR ESSAY

Now you are ready to create the body of your essay. Here is where you must use the best ideas you selected in the pre-writing exercise.

Matt was kind of a loner. Kids sometimes teased him about his hearing aid, but he never lost his temper. That's what made me realize Matt was a very special person. What most amazed me about Matt was that his problems never seemed to get him down.

Later that year, everything changed when Matt began playing basketball. Matt always talked about Michael Jordan and wanted to play like him. Matt practiced every day. At first, he could hardly get the ball in the hoop, and many of the kids made fun of him. But his shooting slowly improved. He worked at it each day, and he got much better too. His hands and feet became much faster, and his eyes were sharp.

PRACTICING WHAT YOU HAVE LEARNED

Now write the body of your own essay.

CONCLUSION TO YOUR ESSAY

Now, bring your essay to an end by relating your conclusion to the overall theme of your essay.

> *By June that school year, Matt's hard work paid off. He became the best basketball player in the school. It was odd to see how, as Matt improved in basketball, fewer and fewer kids seemed to notice his hearing aid. My friendship with Matt taught me an important lesson in life — work hard and persist at something, even if at first you have problems. Most of all, Matt taught me to never put myself down when things don't go my way. Simply work as hard as you can and positive results will come your way. I will never forget my friend Matt.*

PRACTICING WHAT YOU HAVE LEARNED

Now write the conclusion of your essay.

Practice Exercises

At one time or another, we have all had the opportunity to help another person who needed help.

Write a narrative essay about *one* time in your life when you helped another person. Tell what happened and how you felt. Also describe the reactions of the person who was helped.

PRE-WRITING

Directions: Think about a time in your life when you helped someone who really needed help. How did you help the other person? What did you do? How did you feel afterwards? Take time to read and answer the questions that follow. The pre-writing activity will help you get ideas for the story you will write. The pre-writing work will not be scored.

1. **How did you help another person?** Tell about the *where, when, who,* and *how* of your story. Write as many details as you can recall from that situation. Then put a check next to the details you want to use in your essay.

CHAPTER 9: WRITING ABOUT YOUR PERSONAL EXPERIENCES   113

2. **How did you and the other person react?** How did you react to the situation? How did the person you helped react? Write as many details as you think of. Then put a check by the ones that you choose for your essay.

3. **What happened afterwards?** How did your behavior make you feel? Were you glad that you helped? Were you rewarded for your efforts? Did you learn a lesson? Write down what happened afterwards, recalling as many details as you can think of. Then put a check next to the things you want to include in your essay.

A NARRATIVE ABOUT YOUR PERSONAL EXPERIENCES — A Story About Yourself

Now you are going to write a story about a time when you helped another person. The story you write will be scored. Look at the next page. It shows what your best paper must have.

✓ CHECKLIST

I will earn my best score if:

☐ My personal experience essay gives the names of the main people involved.

☐ My personal experience essay tells how I helped another person who needed help.

☐ My personal experience essay tells what actually happened.

☐ My personal experience essay describes my own and the other person's reactions.

☐ My personal experience essay has a beginning, middle, and end.

☐ I use words that make my meaning clear. I do not use the same words over and over.

☐ I try to spell the words correctly.

☐ My sentences and proper names begin with a capital letter.

☐ My sentences end with a period, an exclamation mark, or a question mark.

Directions: You will write a personal experience essay about a time when you helped another person who needed help. Your personal experience essay will tell how you helped that person, how that person reacted, and what happened afterwards. Look back at the pre-writing page in which you answered certain questions, and use the things you checked for your personal experience essay. Your personal experience essay should make sense and have a beginning, a middle, and an end. Be sure to use words that make your meaning clear. Write your personal experience essay on the following page.

Chapter 9: Writing About Your Personal Experiences

Before writing your essay, plan your essay by using the hamburger outline below:

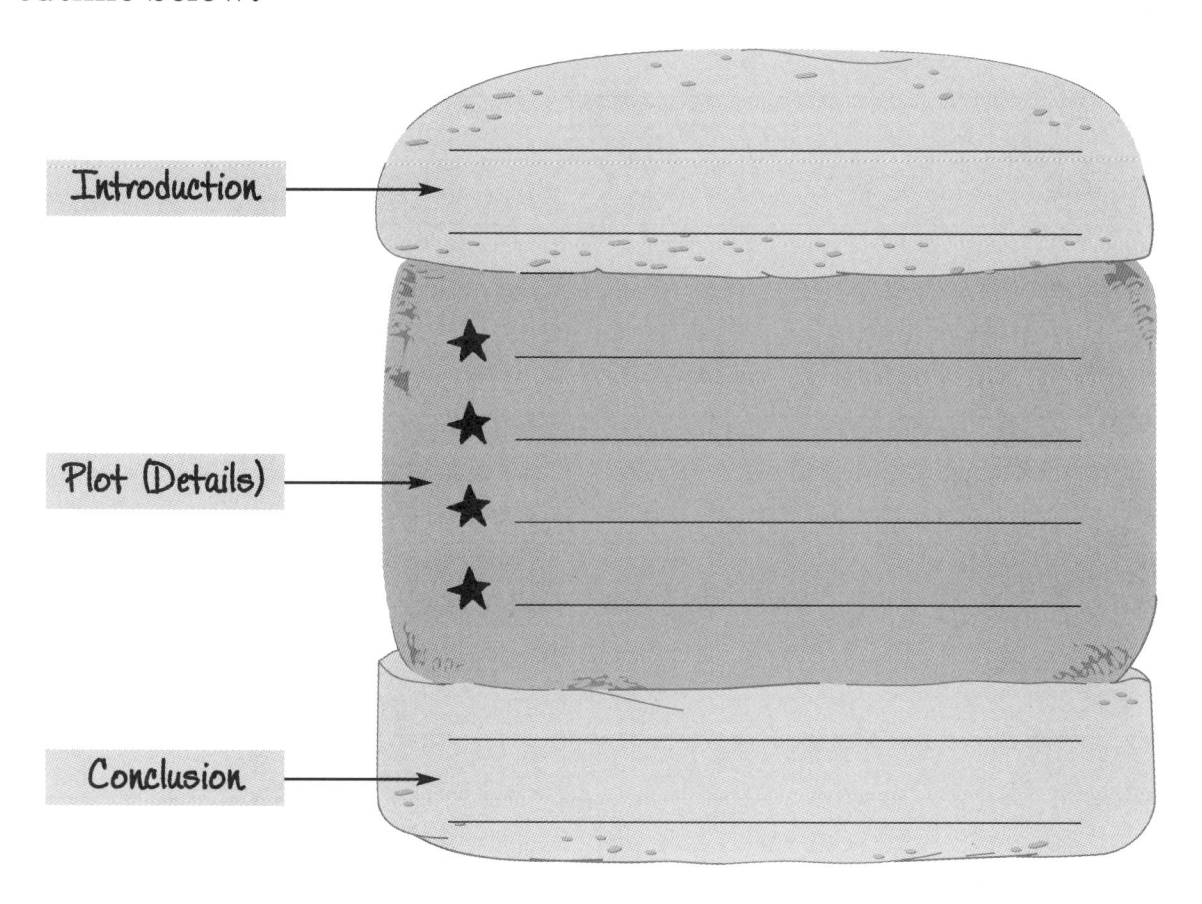

Introduction →

Plot (Details) →
- ★
- ★
- ★
- ★

Conclusion →

Now write your essay below:

When you finish writing your personal experience essay, use the checklist to revise and edit your work. When you have finished checking your essay and you are satisfied with it, you are finished.

CHAPTER 10

WRITING A REPORT

In previous chapters, you learned how to write a fictional narrative and how to write about your personal experiences. A third type of question found on Exercise A of the **Fourth Grade Proficiency Test in Writing** asks you to write a report. A **report** gives a description or explanation of some topic. The purpose of a report is to provide information to the reader about that topic.

You have probably already written a report — such as a book, science or history report — in your classroom or for homework.

★ **Book Report.** In a book report, the writer tells the reader what the book is all about. This includes the name of the author, the title of the book, when and where the events in the book took place, and a brief description of the plot. Most book reports also include the opinion of the writer on how good the book is.

★ **Science Report.** A science report can touch on a variety of different topics. For example, it may tell about a particular animal — what the animal looks like, what it eats, and where it lives.

★ **History Report.** A history report often tells about a famous person, group, or event. For example, a report on the Battle of Fallen Timbers would tell when and where it was fought, who was involved, and why the battle was fought. It might also tell about the effects of the battle.

When you write a report in class, you consult books, encyclopedias, and other sources. However, on the **Fourth Grade Proficiency Test in Writing,** you will not be able to research your topic with outside materials. Instead, the prompt in the question will be an article or some other source of information about your topic.

You will be able to follow along in your booklet as the prompt is read aloud. You will be expected to take notes from the prompt in the pre-writing exercise. You should use these notes to write your report.

Most reports on the **Fourth Grade Proficiency Test in Writing** will ask you either to *describe* or to *explain* something.

- ★ **Descriptive Writing** describes something. You can use descriptive writing to tell about a person, place or thing. Think about the questions a reporter would ask when investigating something — *who, what, when, where, how,* and *why.* Use all five senses to think of all the details you might include. The more precise your language and details are, the stronger an impression will be made on the reader of your report. On the **Fourth Grade Proficiency Test in Writing,** details for your report will be provided in the prompt.

- ★ **Expository Writing** explains something. For example, you could be asked *why* or *how* something took place. To explain why something happened, identify each reason why the event occurred. Provide details from the prompt to explain each reason. To explain how something happened, describe what took place step by step.

HOW TO WRITE A REPORT

Let's suppose you had to write a report about wolves. Read the following excerpts from a book on the subject.

WOLVES
by Seymour Simon

Wolves are the largest members of the dog family, bigger than any wild dogs and most dogs. The wolf looks much like a German shepherd with thick, shaggy fur and bushy tail. The fur is extra thick in winter and is a good protection against rain or snow. Water runs off a wolf's fur the way it runs off a raincoat.

An adult wolf can weigh from 40 to 175 pounds (18 to 80 kilograms) and stretch more than 6 feet (2 meters) from the tip of its nose to the end of its tail. Male wolves are usually larger than female wolves.

Wolves live in packs, but that is just a name for a family of wolves. Packs are usually made up of a leader male and female wolf and their young, along with some close relatives. An average wolf pack has five to eight wolves, but packs can have as few as two or three, or as many as twenty-five wolves.

The members of a pack are usually very friendly with each other. They hunt, travel, eat, and make noises together. Wolves bring bits of food to each other. They baby-sit each other's litters. They run around and play tag with each other and with the pups. They startle each other by hiding and then jumping out.

Wolves' teeth are well-suited for catching and eating other animals. Wolves have powerful jaws. The long, pointed teeth in the front sides of a wolf's jaws are called canines. They are useful for grabbing and holding prey such as a moose.

continued

> Wolves have marvelous hearing. They can hear other wolves howling from three or four miles away. They can locate mice by the squeals they make even when the rodents are beneath a snowpack. Like bats and dolphins, wolves can also hear high-pitched sounds well above the range of human hearing. Scientists believe wolves hunt small prey more by sound than by smell or sight. Larger prey is often found by scent or by chance encounters.
>
> Wolves can run for miles without tiring when hunting moose, elk or other large prey. Wolves have strong muscles, and their legs are long and almost spindly. Like dogs, and most other animals, wolves run on their toes. This makes their legs even longer and lets them take long steps, so that they can run fast. Wolves seem to glide effortlessly when they run, almost like the shadow of a cloud drifting along the ground.
>
> Wolves hunt animals in different ways. A single wolf will hunt by itself for small prey including mice, rabbits, squirrels, beavers, ducks, geese, and even fish when available. But much of their prey are large animals such as deer, elk, moose, caribou, musk oxen and bighorn sheep. Most of these are hard to catch and can be dangerous when cornered, so wolves hunt them in packs. Wolves hunt moose by trying to encircle them and bring them to a standstill.

This reading selection describes wolves and explains how they hunt. Readers who are good fact finders will look back at this information and read it again.

PRE-WRITING SECTION

Now you are ready to take notes for writing your report. This pre-writing work will not be scored. However, the notes will be used to complete your writing exercises. The pre-writing section will have topics on cards to help you organize the information in the article. You must be able to identify important information and **classify** — arrange, organize and sort — the information into the correct cards.

On the actual test, you will have several blank cards in your test booklet. Each card will identify a topic at the top. You will need to complete the rest of the card with the correct information. This information will be found in the prompt (*reading selection*). Now let's examine the steps you must use in order to complete each note card:

★ Look at the topic identified at the top of the card. The topic tells you what information you will need to complete each card.

★ Read through the article (*prompt*) again for information about each topic.

★ Then, list all the important facts about the topic on that note card.

For example, for this reading you might have been given three cards. The first of these cards has been completed for you.

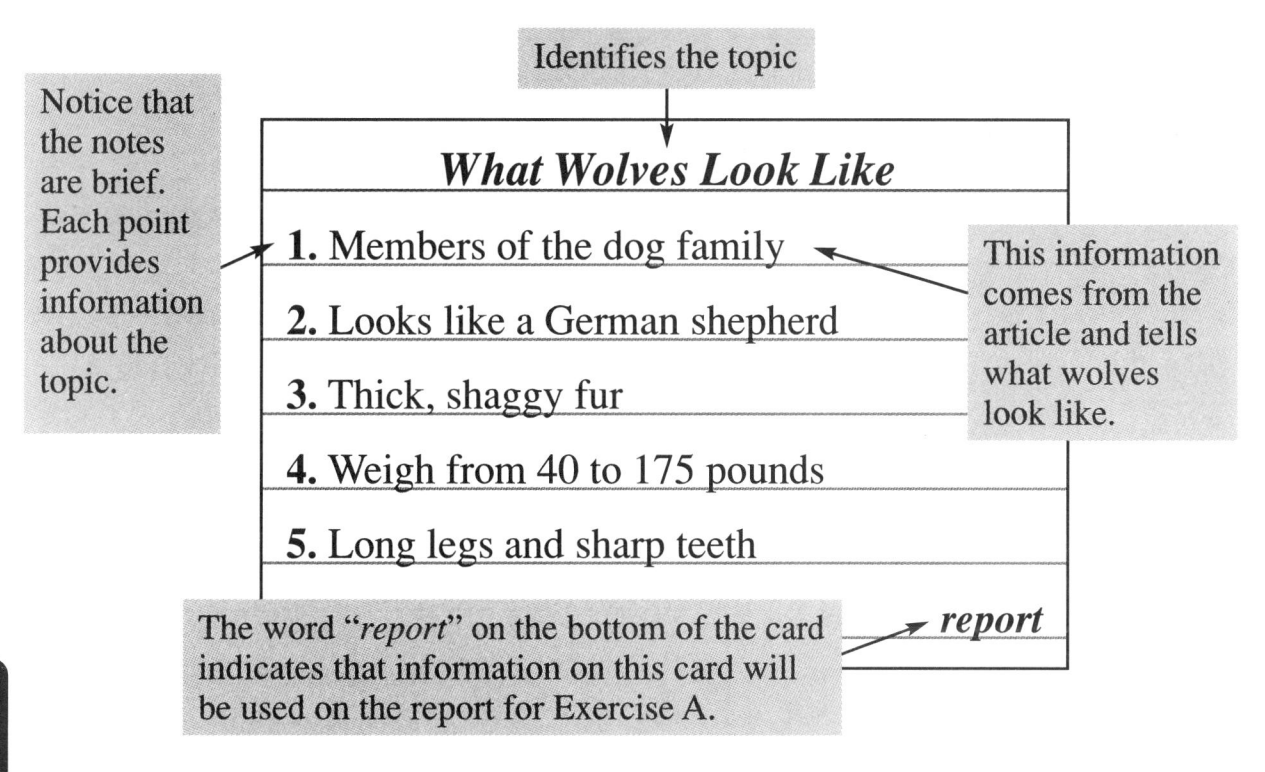

Notice that the notes are brief. Each point provides information about the topic.

Identifies the topic

What Wolves Look Like

1. Members of the dog family
2. Looks like a German shepherd
3. Thick, shaggy fur
4. Weigh from 40 to 175 pounds
5. Long legs and sharp teeth

This information comes from the article and tells what wolves look like.

report

The word "*report*" on the bottom of the card indicates that information on this card will be used on the report for Exercise A.

Now that you have seen how a completed note card should look, complete the other two cards. Remember, these are in note form and will help you to organize the information you will use in your report.

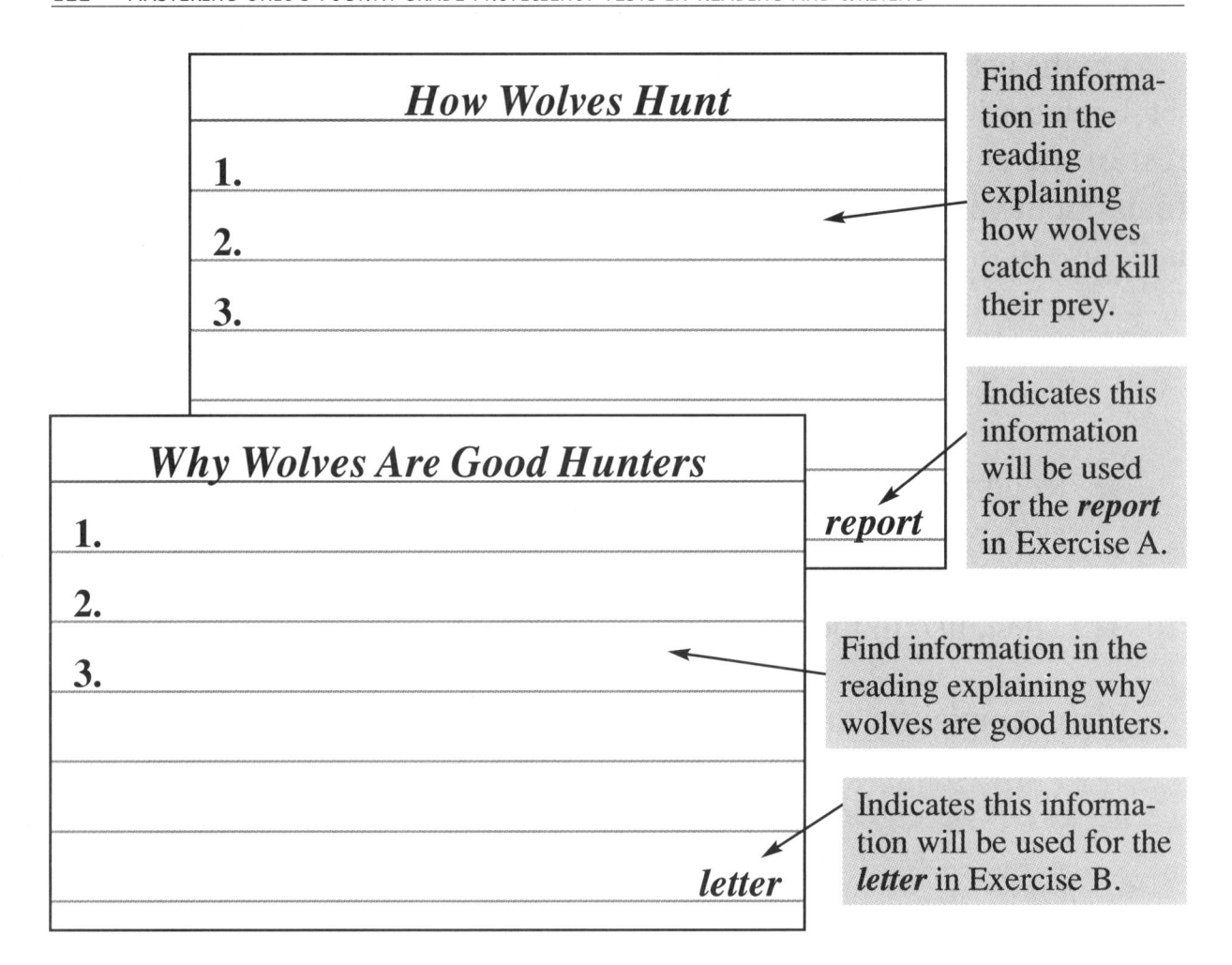

How Wolves Hunt

1.
2.
3.

Find information in the reading explaining how wolves catch and kill their prey.

*Indicates this information will be used for the **report** in Exercise A.*

report

Why Wolves Are Good Hunters

1.
2.
3.

Find information in the reading explaining why wolves are good hunters.

*Indicates this information will be used for the **letter** in Exercise B.*

letter

Now you are ready to complete **two** writing exercises about wolves. First, you will be asked to write a report describing wolves and how they hunt. Two of the note cards have the word "***report***" written on them. Use the information found on these cards in your report to complete **Exercise A.**

On the test, you would also be asked to complete a second writing activity — **Exercise B.** In this example, this exercise might require you to write a letter to a friend explaining why wolves are good hunters. You would use the note card with the word ***letter*** for this second activity.

You will learn more about how to go about writing letters in the next chapter. Some of your note cards may be marked "***report / letter.***" This means the information on that note card can be used both in **Exercise A** for your report, and in **Exercise B** for your letter. Now let's look at how to go about writing your report for **Exercise A.**

WRITING YOUR REPORT

The test itself will say something like the following:

> In this section, you will be given directions on what to write for your report. These directions are followed by a checklist that will help remind you about what you must include in your report to earn the best score.
>
> **Directions:** Write a report describing wolves and how they hunt. Be sure to use many facts in your report. Write your report so that it makes sense and is complete.
>
> Look at the box below. It shows what your best paper must have.
>
> ### ☑ CHECKLIST
>
> **I will earn my best score if:**
> - ❑ My report tells what wolves look like.
> - ❑ My report describes how wolves hunt.
> - ❑ My report is complete.
> - ❑ My report tells about wolves in my own words.
> - ❑ I use words that make my meaning clear in my report. I do not use the same words over and over.
> - ❑ I try to spell the words correctly.
> - ❑ My sentences and proper names begin with a capital letter.
> - ❑ My sentences end with a period, an exclamation mark, or a question mark.

Just like a fictional or personal narrative, a report should have an introduction, a body, and a conclusion. You can use your note cards as the outline for the body of your report. You can also make a separate outline using the hamburger method, or simply jot down your ideas for an introduction and conclusion before you write. Then write out your report, putting the information on the note cards into your own words.

A MODEL REPORT

The following is an example of a report for **Exercise A**, in which you are asked to describe wolves and how they hunt. The introduction, the first paragraph of the body, and the conclusion have all been done for you. You should complete the second paragraph of the report dealing with how wolves hunt.

Try to open your report with a surprising fact or thought-provoking question.	Did you know that one of nature's best hunters can also be a fun-loving, playful, and friendly animal? This report will describe the wolf, and tell about how wolves hunt and kill their prey.
The introduction tells the reader the topic of your report.	
This paragraph describes how wolves look.	The closest animal relative to the wolf is the dog. In fact, many wolves actually look something like German shepherds. A typical wolf has thick, shaggy fur. Wolves usually weigh from 40 to 75 pounds. They have long legs and sharp teeth.
In this section write a paragraph describing how wolves hunt.	_____ _____ _____ _____ _____ _____
The conclusion signals to your reader that the report has come to an end. Most writers summarize their main points or present some general lesson in the conclusion.	Wolves live by hunting, and this report has shown how their typical features and habits help them to hunt. While they look much like dogs, wolves are wild animals that survive by killing other animals. By acting together they can even hunt animals larger than themselves.

Practice Exercises

WRITING A REPORT

Directions: Read the following article about the Native American tribes of the Great Lakes.

NATIVE AMERICAN TRIBES OF THE GREAT LAKES

Long before the voyages of Christopher Columbus, the tribes of the Great Lakes region had developed lifestyles that made use of the resources nature made available to them.

Most of the villages of the Great Lakes tribes were built near rivers or lakes. Canoes were used for transportation and to search for food. Usually, the men did the hunting, fishing, and making of canoes. They used natural materials, such as rocks and plant fibers, to make tools and weapons. They used spears, hooks and nets to fish in the waters of the Great Lakes. Bows and arrows, spears and clubs were used to kill deer, rabbits, moose, squirrels, beavers, ducks and turkeys. Some meat and fish were preserved and stored for later use in the winter.

A Native American line-fishing from his canoe.

Women gathered berries, nuts and other wild plants. Children helped gather berries and wild rice. Women were also in charge of growing corn, squash, beans, potatoes and other vegetables. Corn was a major food in their diet. Women crushed corn in stone bowls to make flour used in making breads or stews.

continued

Men cleared the land for planting by setting fire to the trees in an area. After the trees were burned down, ashes from the fire were mixed with the soil. Then the crops were planted, usually by the women. After 15 to 20 years, the soil became exhausted from continued planting. A village would then move to a new location.

The Great Lakes tribes depended on the animals they hunted for food and clothing. Most tribes made skirts, moccasins, leggings and clothes from the skins of deer and other animals. They used sharp porcupine needles to create designs. Tribe members sometimes tattooed their faces and decorated themselves with feathers and shells. Tribes of the Great Lakes collected shells to make **wampum.** The wampum beads were strung together to make belts, ornaments and money.

Religion was important in the lives of the Great Lakes tribes. They worshiped a Great Spirit believed to be in all animals and objects. They also believed in gods of the sky, woods and lakes. A tribal medicine man or woman helped people communicate with the spirit world.

Tribes of the Great Lakes believed people could not own the things of nature, such as land, forests and animals. They belonged to everyone. Everything was shared with tribe members. If members of the village did not work together to store enough food for winter, its members would face starvation. They believed all people were part of the Great Spirit, and that tribal leaders, known as chiefs, should listen to everyone.

Warfare was closely related to religion. A tribe frequently went to war if a member was killed by another tribe. It was believed the spirit of the dead member could not rest until revenge was taken. War party members would bathe and not eat for several days to purify themselves. Often, they would make a surprise attack on their enemy.

This article described the lifestyles and beliefs of the tribes of the Great Lakes. Readers who are good fact finders will look back at the information and read it again.

PRE-WRITING

Directions: The topics on the cards can help you organize the information you will use in your writing activities.

How the Tribes Hunted and Fished

1. _____
2. _____
3. _____

report

How the Tribes Grew Food

1. _____
2. _____
3. _____

report

How the Tribes Dressed

1. _____
2. _____
3. _____

report

Religious Beliefs and Community Values

1.

2.

3.

report / letter

Warfare: How The Tribes Fought

1.

2.

3.

report / letter

Look through the article on the Great Lakes tribes for information about each topic. Then, on each note card, list all the important facts about the topic. From the information you write on the cards you will be asked to do **Exercise A** (*writing a report*) and **Exercise B** (*writing a letter*).

Now you are ready to write a report about the Native American tribes of the Great Lakes. Write a report describing their major activities and beliefs. Some of your note cards have the word *report* written on them. Use the information on these cards in your report. Some cards are also marked *letter.* These cards would be used to help you complete **Exercise B** — writing a letter.

NOTE: For this activity, you should focus only on doing **Exercise A: Report.** In the following chapter, you will learn about writing letters.

EXERCISE A: WRITING A REPORT

The writing in **Exercise A** will be scored. Look at the box below. It shows to do your best work.

✔ CHECKLIST

I will earn my best score if:

- ☐ My response stays on the topic.
- ☐ My report describes the major activities of the Great Lakes tribes.
- ☐ My report tells about the major beliefs of the Great Lakes tribes.
- ☐ My report is complete.
- ☐ My report tells about the Great Lakes tribes in my own words.
- ☐ I use words that make my meaning clear in my report. I do not use the same words over and over.
- ☐ I try to spell the words correctly.
- ☐ My sentences and proper names begin with a capital letter.
- ☐ My sentences end with a period, an exclamation mark, or a question mark.

When you finish writing your report, use the checklist to revise and edit your work. When you have finished checking your report and you are satisfied with it, you are finished.

CHAPTER 11

WRITING LETTERS, JOURNALS AND DIRECTIONS

The test may ask you to communicate information by **writing a letter, keeping a journal or giving directions.** These types of writings are found on **Exercise B** of the test. Let's start by looking at how to write a letter. Later, we will examine journal writing, and giving directions.

WRITING LETTERS

Although we use letters for a variety of purposes, they all follow a common form with a greeting, body, and closing.

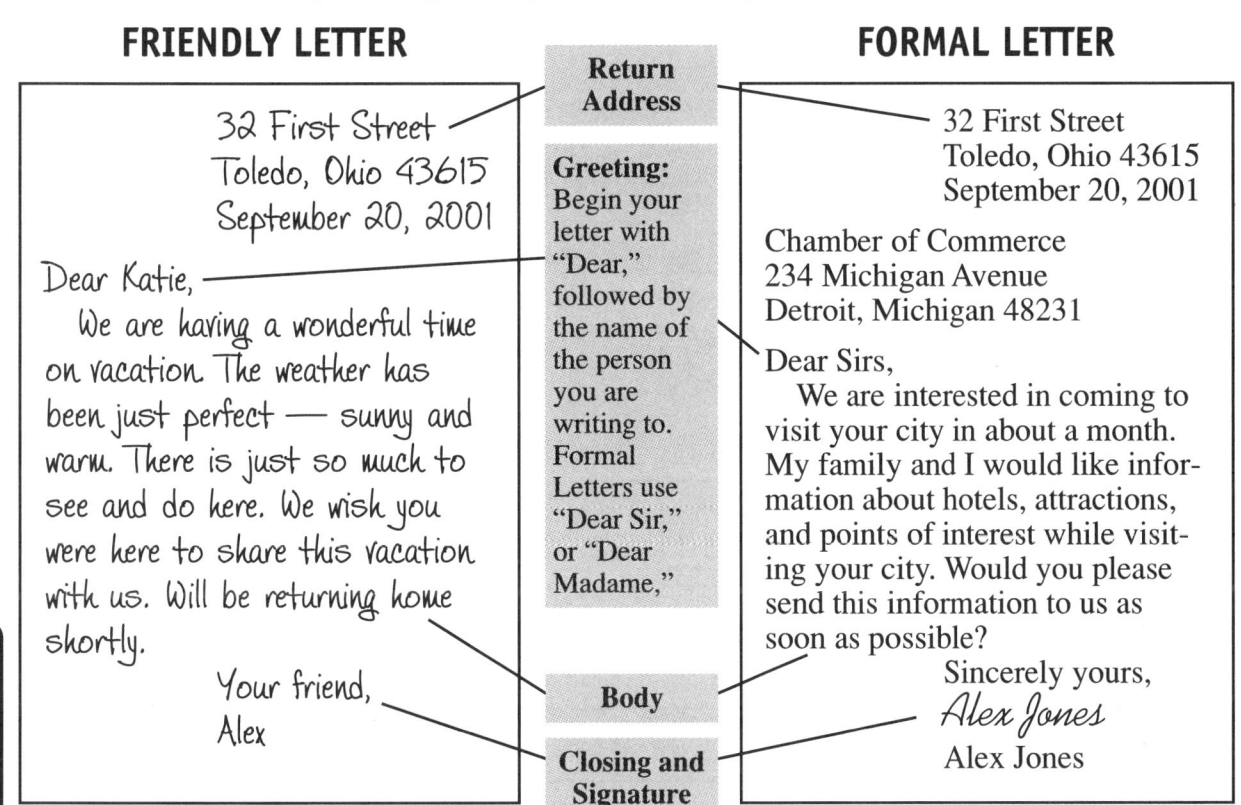

FRIENDLY LETTER

32 First Street
Toledo, Ohio 43615
September 20, 2001

Dear Katie,

　We are having a wonderful time on vacation. The weather has been just perfect — sunny and warm. There is just so much to see and do here. We wish you were here to share this vacation with us. Will be returning home shortly.

　　　　Your friend,
　　　　Alex

Return Address

Greeting: Begin your letter with "Dear," followed by the name of the person you are writing to. Formal Letters use "Dear Sir," or "Dear Madame,"

Body

Closing and Signature

FORMAL LETTER

32 First Street
Toledo, Ohio 43615
September 20, 2001

Chamber of Commerce
234 Michigan Avenue
Detroit, Michigan 48231

Dear Sirs,

　We are interested in coming to visit your city in about a month. My family and I would like information about hotels, attractions, and points of interest while visiting your city. Would you please send this information to us as soon as possible?

　　　　Sincerely yours,
　　　　Alex Jones
　　　　Alex Jones

PRACTICE WRITING A LETTER

Now you try it. Suppose you had a pen pal who lived somewhere in Asia. Write your pen pal a letter about an event that took place recently in your school or community.

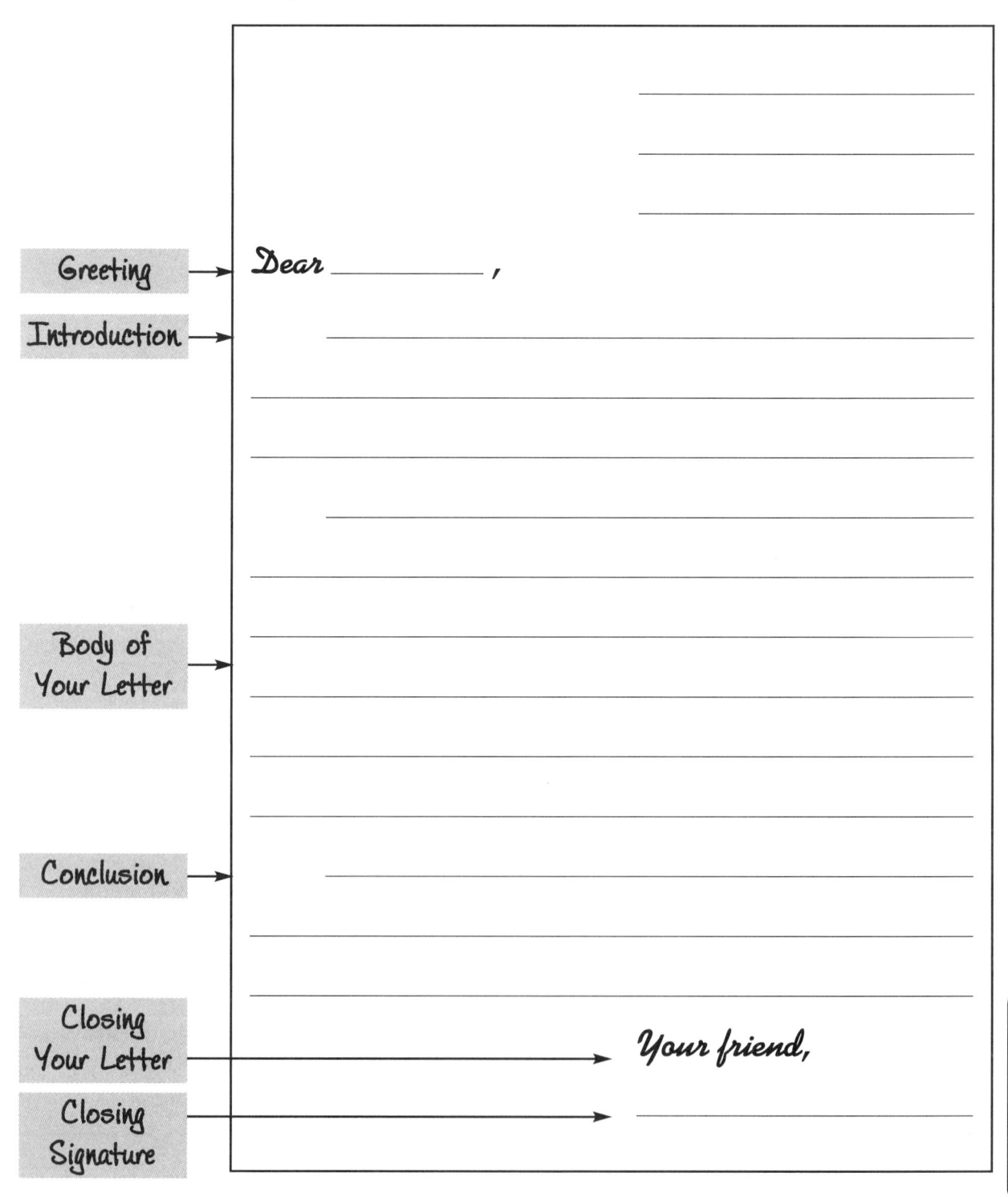

- Greeting → Dear _____,
- Introduction →
- Body of Your Letter →
- Conclusion →
- Closing Your Letter → Your friend,
- Closing Signature →

CHAPTER 11: WRITING LETTERS, JOURNALS AND DIRECTIONS   133

Some of the special types of letters you may be asked to write on the test include a letter to an editor, a thank-you note, and an invitation. Let's examine each of these types of letters.

WRITING A LETTER TO THE EDITOR

People write letters to the editors of newspapers when they want to express their views about a topic. A letter printed in a newspaper may be read by hundreds or even thousands of people.

HELPFUL HINTS

A letter to the editor should clearly state your viewpoint. It is a form of *persuasive essay,* intended to convince others. The body of the letter should present logical reasons why the reader should adopt your view.

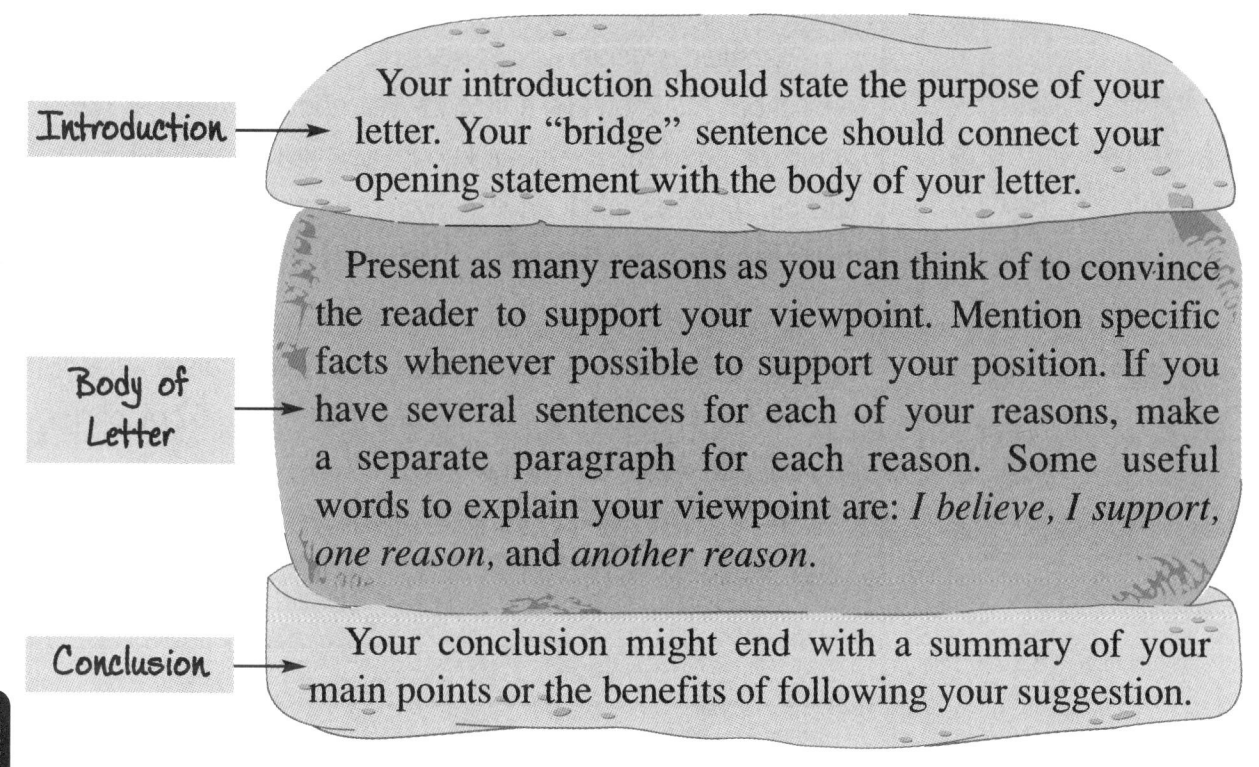

Introduction → Your introduction should state the purpose of your letter. Your "bridge" sentence should connect your opening statement with the body of your letter.

Body of Letter → Present as many reasons as you can think of to convince the reader to support your viewpoint. Mention specific facts whenever possible to support your position. If you have several sentences for each of your reasons, make a separate paragraph for each reason. Some useful words to explain your viewpoint are: *I believe, I support, one reason*, and *another reason.*

Conclusion → Your conclusion might end with a summary of your main points or the benefits of following your suggestion.

Suppose you are asked to write a letter to the editor about whether skateboards should be permitted on school playgrounds. Following is the letter of one student who opposed the use of skateboards.

A MODEL LETTER TO THE EDITOR

The introduction states the purpose of the letter.

The bridge sentence connects the introduction to the body of the letter.

Notice how the paragraphs in the body of the letter present reasons to convince the reader.

Notice how the conclusion sums up the author's viewpoint.

> 32 First Street
> Toledo, Ohio 43615
> September 20, 2001
>
> Toledo Gazette
> To the Editor:
>
> I believe our community should not permit the use of skateboards on the playground at our elementary school. I oppose the use of skateboards on school playgrounds for a number of reasons.
>
> One reason why I believe skateboards should not be permitted on school playgrounds is that a student on a skateboard might run into another student by accident. This could cause needless injuries.
>
> Another reason I oppose the use of skateboards on school playgrounds concerns the additional noise that would be created. Everyone knows how noisy skateboards can be. With so much noise, other students may not hear their teacher's instructions if students are skateboarding at the same time.
>
> In conclusion, I believe that to prevent unnecessary accidents, the use of skateboards on the school playground should not be permitted.
>
> Sincerely yours,
>
> *Alan Jones*
> Alan Jones

PRACTICE WRITING A LETTER TO THE EDITOR

Now you try it. Write to your local newspaper editor explaining why you favor or oppose having a longer school year and a shorter summer vacation.

CHAPTER 11: WRITING LETTERS, JOURNALS AND DIRECTIONS   **135**

- Greeting → *To the Editor:*
- Introduction →
- Body of Letter →
- Conclusion →
- Closing the Letter → *Sincerely yours,*
- Closing Signature →

WRITING A THANK-YOU LETTER

We often write a thank-you letter to show someone our appreciation after receiving a gift, hospitality, or some other form of generosity.

HELPFUL HINTS

A thank-you letter should express your true feelings. It should not focus on the gift or favor itself. The letter need not be long, and may be only one or two paragraphs.

Introduction. Introduce your letter by stating what you are grateful for. Express your gratitude in an enthusiastic, appreciative way.

Body. The body is where you should elaborate on your appreciation. Mention specifically what pleased you about the gift, favor or kindness. Describe why you like the item, how you are going to use it, or something you particularly enjoyed about your stay at your friend's house. Never express more than you really feel. A simple thank you often goes a long way in showing your appreciation. You might also say something about your return home, or how you and your family have been since you last met.

Conclusion. Conclude by writing one or two sentences that are unrelated to the object of your gratitude. Here you should express affection for the person, promise to see the person soon, send greetings to other family members, or say something else nice about the person to whom you are writing the letter.

PRACTICE WRITING A THANK-YOU LETTER

Let's practice what you have just learned about writing a thank-you letter. Pretend you have to write a thank-you letter to a friend who visited you at home while you were recovering from an illness.

CHAPTER 11: WRITING LETTERS, JOURNALS AND DIRECTIONS   **137**

Greeting → Dear _____ ,

Introduction →

Body of Letter →

Conclusion →

Closing the Letter → Your friend,

Closing Signature →

WRITING AN INVITATION

Another type of letter you might be asked to write on the **Fourth Grade Proficiency Test in Writing** is an invitation. This could be either a formal or friendly letter, depending on the occasion and the person to whom you are writing.

HELPFUL HINTS

Important events in our lives are often celebrated with a social gathering. Invitations are used for these occasions. These events include dinners, cook-outs, fund-raising events, birthdays, school events, baby showers, engagements, weddings, meetings and receptions.

Introduction. In an invitation you should state the occasion — for example an open house, dinner, dance or birthday party.

Body. The body of the invitation is where you provide the date (*month, day*) and time (*include A.M. or P.M.*). Include the address with directions if the location of the celebration is difficult to find. Mention if refreshments will be served. It is also necessary to mention the preferred dress — formal, informal, casual or costume. Additional information might include an alternate date in case of rain.

Conclusion. Conclude by indicating a telephone number and date by which the person being invited is to respond. An invitation often ends by expressing your anticipated pleasure at seeing the person, such as "*I look forward to seeing you at the party, where we can catch up on old news.*"

PRACTICE WRITING AN INVITATION

Let's practice what you have just learned about writing an invitation. Write a letter to a friend of yours inviting him or her to a costume party on Halloween night.

CHAPTER 11: WRITING LETTERS, JOURNALS AND DIRECTIONS **139**

Greeting → Dear _____ ,

Introduction →

Body of Letter →

Conclusion →

Closing the Letter → Your friend,

Closing Signature →

UNLAWFUL TO PHOTOCOPY

KEEPING A JOURNAL

The test may also ask you to write a journal entry. A **journal** is a record of your own observations. Journals help you to keep track of events. People keep journals for a variety of reasons. For example, the most popular journal is probably the *diary* — a day-to-day recording of events. Professional reporters keep journals too — to recall facts to use in their articles. Writers keep journals to practice and improve their writing and thinking skills. A journal may help you to keep track of particular events that interest you and are reported in the news or on television. A journal may help you preserve your memories or serve as a source for ideas.

HELPFUL HINTS

The length of time you keep a journal can vary. You might keep a journal for only a few days or for many years. In addition, how often you make a journal entry may also vary. You might make an entry several times a day, once a week, or only occasionally. In general, every journal entry is recorded along with the date on which it is written. For example, the following imaginary journal entries might have been written by early pioneers of Ohio.

A MODEL JOURNAL

DATE	Journal Entry
Jan. 17, 1793	The weather is bitterly cold. Our supplies are low and we don't know if we'll make it through this winter. We've decided to organize a hunting party, but are afraid of hostile tribes.
Jan. 20, 1793	We have just heard that General Wayne and his troops are not far from here. That means we can go hunt without worrying about tribal attacks.
Jan. 25, 1793	I am sad to say that little Jim is very sick from lack of food. His fever is high and his mother is worried. We melted some snow to make a weak soup with potatoes.

PRACTICE WRITING JOURNAL ENTRIES

Let's practice what you have just learned about making journal entries. Pretend you are on a trip visiting another country or another part of the United States. Make journal entries for three days recording your impressions of the place you have been visiting.

DATE	Journal Entry

GIVING DIRECTIONS

Exercise B of the **Fourth Grade Proficiency Test in Writing** may require you to write a set of directions showing the reader how to get somewhere or to do something. You may, for example, read some information in the test prompt and then be asked to turn this information into instructions for someone else. The key to writing directions is to break down what has to be done into a series of simple steps. Then clearly communicate these steps, one at a time, to your reader.

HELPFUL HINTS

When giving directions, help the reader with clear instructions on what to do and how to do it.

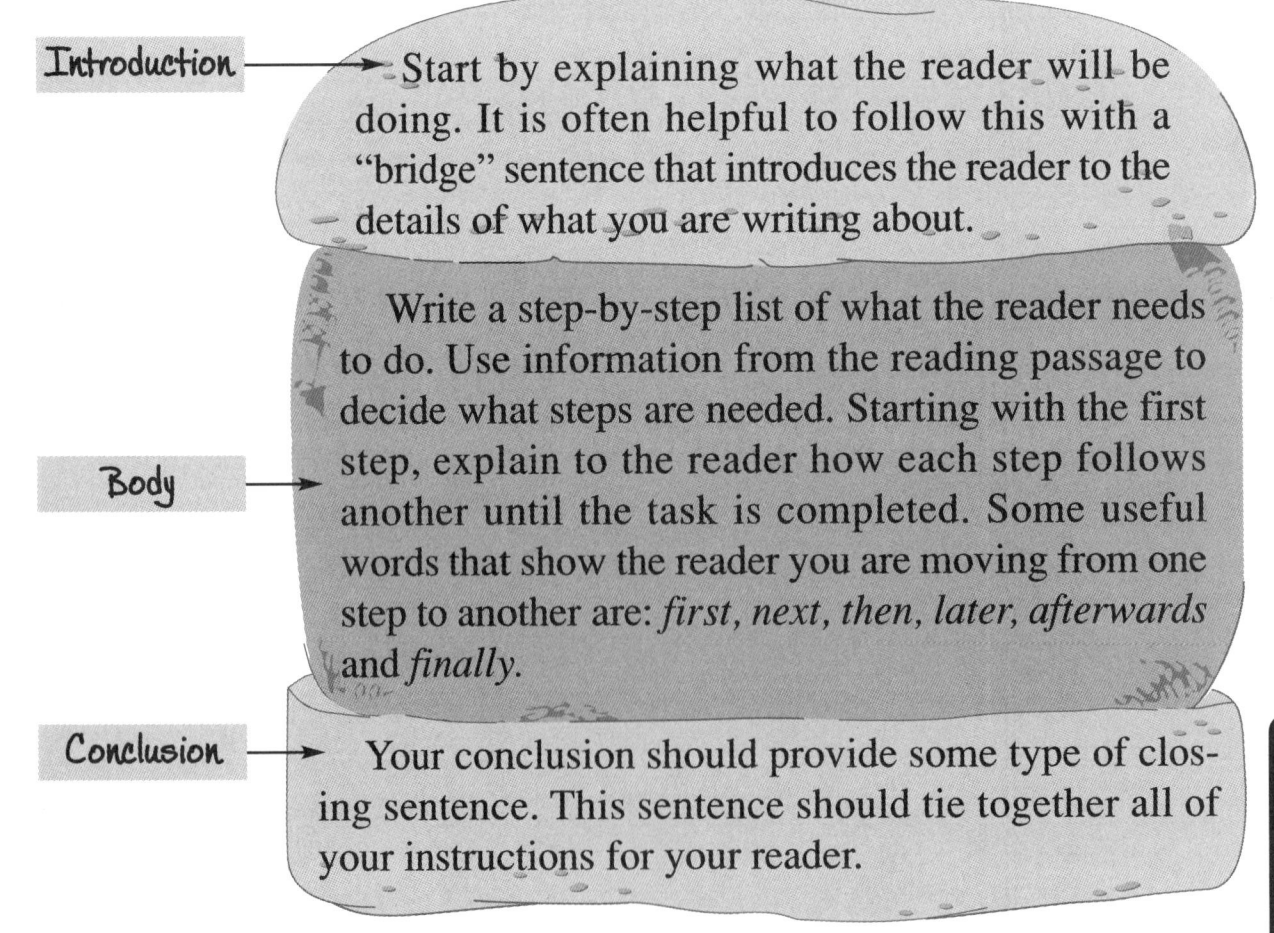

Introduction → Start by explaining what the reader will be doing. It is often helpful to follow this with a "bridge" sentence that introduces the reader to the details of what you are writing about.

Body → Write a step-by-step list of what the reader needs to do. Use information from the reading passage to decide what steps are needed. Starting with the first step, explain to the reader how each step follows another until the task is completed. Some useful words that show the reader you are moving from one step to another are: *first, next, then, later, afterwards* and *finally*.

Conclusion → Your conclusion should provide some type of closing sentence. This sentence should tie together all of your instructions for your reader.

CHAPTER 11: WRITING LETTERS, JOURNALS AND DIRECTIONS

Suppose you are asked to give someone directions to your house. Following is an example of how one student provided directions to her house.

A MODEL SET OF DIRECTIONS

The introduction tells the reader what the passage will explain.

Following are the directions for finding my house located at 75 Fox Lane. If you follow my directions carefully, you should reach my house in about an hour.

The bridge sentence lets the reader know what to expect

First, take Route 680 going east. Then, get off Route 680 at the exit sign reading: Pleasant Hill Road. When you come to that sign, turn left. After driving two blocks you will come to a hill. Drive up the hill and continue past two traffic lights until you come to Fox Lane.

Step-by-step instructions take the reader through each part of the directions.

Finally, make a right turn at Fox Lane. Our home is the second house on the right. Some people have trouble seeing the street sign for Fox Lane, since it is partly hidden by a large tree. You can recognize Fox Lane by the gas station on the corner.

The conclusion ties it all together for the reader.

If you follow these directions carefully, I'm sure you will have no trouble finding my house. I look forward to seeing you soon.

PRACTICE GIVING WRITTEN DIRECTIONS

Now you try it. Write a series of step-by-step directions for making a peanut butter and jelly sandwich.

Introduction →

Body →

Conclusion →

CHAPTER 11: WRITING LETTERS, JOURNALS AND DIRECTIONS 145

Practice Exercises

Write a friendly letter to an imaginary pen pal, George, about what you did last summer. In your letter, tell about what you did during the summer. Be sure your letter includes both good and bad events. Write your letter using this and the next page.

Dear George,

Your friend,

CHAPTER 12

CHECKING YOUR UNDERSTANDING

Now that you have read about various types of writing, let's see how well you understand what you have learned. In this chapter, you will have an opportunity to practice with a complete model **Grade 4 Proficiency Test in Writing.** It will have a writing prompt, a pre-writing activity, and two writing assignments.

You will have about **60 minutes** to complete this section. Try to time yourself. This will help you get an idea of how long it takes you to complete questions similar to what you may find on the actual test.

Below is an illustration of a newspaper headline about a reward of $500 that you recently received.

The Daily Ohio Observer

Vol. 1.9 No. 24 — First Edition

Fourth Grader Receives $500 Reward

Now you will do some thinking and planning for a story about this headline. You will make up and write a story about yourself, and then you will write a letter about it.

PRE-WRITING

Directions: Look at the newspaper headline. What might have been the reason for the reward? Who gave you the reward? How are you going to spend your money? Take time to read and answer the questions that follow about the newspaper headline. The pre-writing activity will help you get ideas for the story that you will make up. The pre-writing work will not be scored.

1. **What was the reason for the reward?** Write as many reasons as you can think of for receiving a reward. Then put a check next to the reasons that you want to use in your story.

2. **Who gave the reward?** Think about who might be giving the reward. What might have prompted the person to offer a reward? Write as many possible donors as you can think of. Then put a check by the ones that you choose for your story.

3. **How will you use the reward?** Write down some of the ways you might use the reward money. Write as many possibilities down as you can think of. Then put a check next to the things you would best spend the money on.

Exercise A:

A FICTIONAL NARRATIVE — A Story You Make Up

Now you are going to do two writing activities. First you are going to make up or invent a story involving yourself, based on the newspaper headline, and then you are going to write an invitation to a friend for a party your parents are giving in your honor for receiving the reward.

The story you write will be scored. Look at the box below. It shows what your best paper must have.

✓ CHECKLIST

I will earn my best score if:

- ❑ My made-up story gives the reasons for the reward.
- ❑ My made-up story tells who gave me the reward.
- ❑ My made-up story tells how I am going to spend the reward money.
- ❑ My made-up story has a beginning, middle and end.
- ❑ I use words that make my meaning clear. I do not use the same words over and over.
- ❑ I try to spell the words correctly.
- ❑ My sentences and proper names begin with a capital letter.
- ❑ My sentences end with a period, an exclamation mark, or a question mark.

Directions: You will make up a story about the newspaper headline and why you received the reward. Look back at the pre-writing page in which you answered certain questions, and use the things you checked for your story. Your story should make sense and have a beginning, a middle and an end. Be sure to use words that make your meaning clear. Write your story on the following page.

Now write your fictional narrative.

When you finish writing your narrative, use the checklist to revise and edit your work. When you have finished checking your narrative and you are satisfied with it, you may go ahead to the second activity, **Exercise B.**

Exercise B:

A LETTER OF INVITATION

The letter of invitation you write will be scored. Look at the box below. The box shows what your invitation must have to get your best score.

✔ CHECKLIST

I will earn my best score if:

- ☐ My letter of invitation tells the reason for the party.
- ☐ My letter of invitation gives details about when and where the party will be held.
- ☐ My letter of invitation is complete.
- ☐ I use the form of a letter with a greeting, a body and a closing.
- ☐ I use words that make my meaning clear in my letter.
- ☐ I try to spell the words correctly.
- ☐ My sentences and proper names begin with a capital letter.
- ☐ My sentences end with a period, an exclamation mark, or a question mark.

Directions: Write a letter to a friend inviting him or her to a party being given by your parents in your honor for what you did to get the reward. Look back at your pre-writing page for ideas. You may decide to use one of the ideas that you wrote down but did not use in your story. Write your letter on the following page.

Dear _____,

Your friend,

When you finish writing your letter of invitation, use the checklist to revise and edit your work. Take out your book to read or other work to do at your desk when you have finished checking your work and you are satisfied with it. Or you may go back to your first writing, your narrative, and work on it some more.

Final Practice Tests in Reading and Writing

A Practice Test in Reading

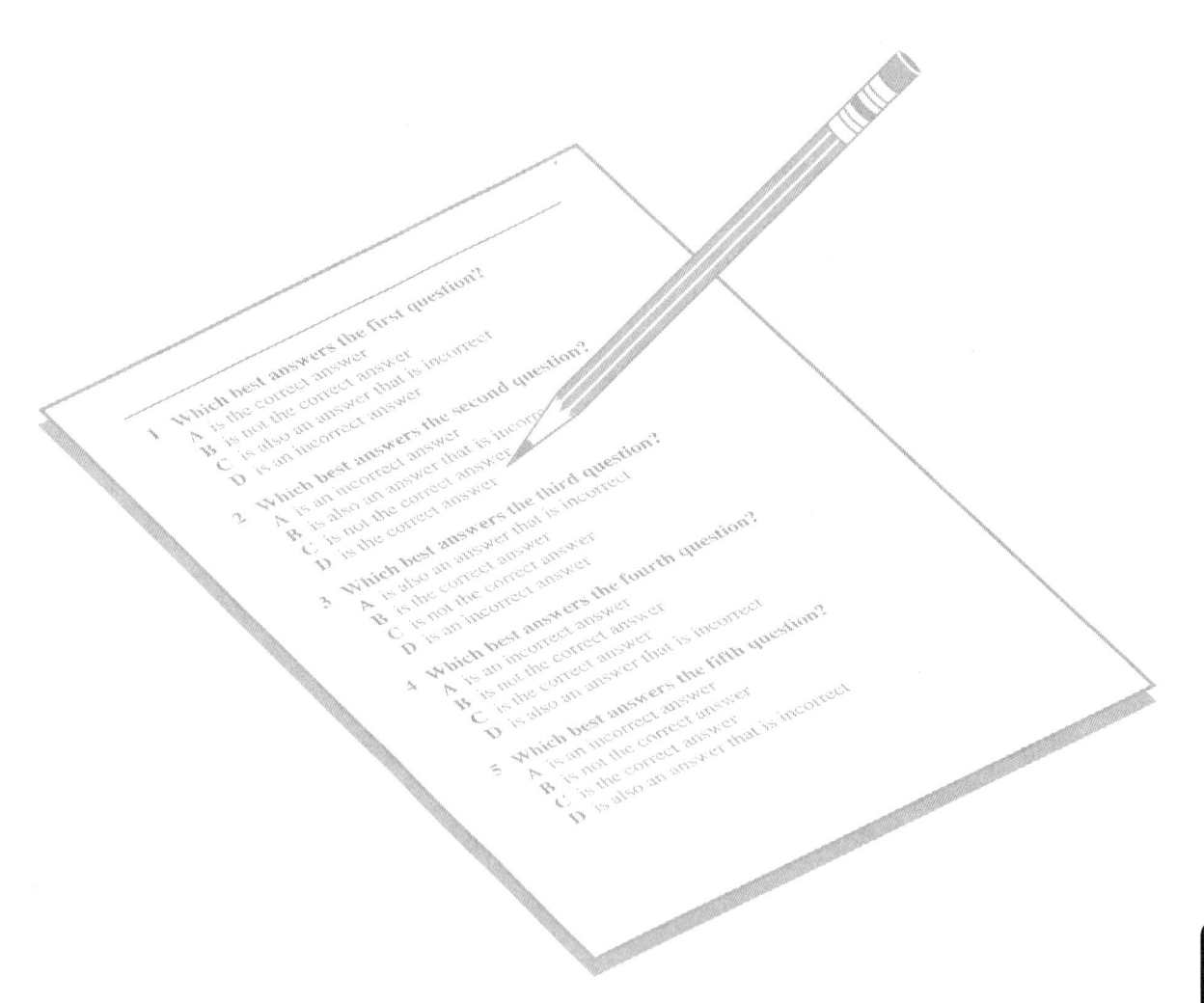

1. Which best answers the first question?
   A is the correct answer
   B is not the correct answer
   C is also an answer that is incorrect
   D is an incorrect answer

2. Which best answers the second question?
   A is an incorrect answer
   B is also an answer that is incorrect
   C is not the correct answer
   D is the correct answer

3. Which best answers the third question?
   A is also an answer that is incorrect
   B is the correct answer
   C is not the correct answer
   D is an incorrect answer

4. Which best answers the fourth question?
   A is an incorrect answer
   B is not the correct answer
   C is the correct answer
   D is also an answer that is incorrect

5. Which best answers the fifth question?
   A is an incorrect answer
   B is not the correct answer
   C is the correct answer
   D is also an answer that is incorrect

DIRECTIONS FOR THE READING SECTION OF THE PRACTICE TEST

You will now take the reading section of the practice test. The test consists of three different types of questions: multiple-choice, short answer, and extended response.

There are several important things to remember:

- ★ Read each selection carefully. You may go back to each reading selection as often as necessary.

- ★ Read each question carefully. Think about what is being asked. If a graph or other diagram goes with the question, read it carefully to help you answer the question. Then choose or write the answer that you think is best.

- ★ When you are asked to write an answer, write it neatly and clearly on the lines or in the box provided.

- ★ When you are asked to select an answer, make sure you fill in the circle next to the correct answer.

- ★ If you do not know the answer to a question, skip it and go on. You may return to it later if you have time.

- ★ If you finish the test early, you may check over your work.

- ★ Write or mark your answers directly on the paper.

- ★ When your reach the word **STOP** in your test booklet, do not go on until you are told to turn the page.

Ask your teacher if you have any questions about what you are to do. If you are taking this test in class, close your booklet when you are finished. Now turn to page 158.

Directions: Read the selection and answer the questions.

HOW BIG MOUTH WRESTLED THE GIANT

There was once a lad known for his bragging. Everyone called him Big Mouth. Whenever Big Mouth spoke about anything he saw, it became the biggest, or the ugliest, or the best ever. Big Mouth himself was the bravest, smartest young man in the whole countryside — according to Big Mouth. But, of course, no one believed him at all.

Big Mouth was always bragging about how he would fight the giant who lived in the woods and make him cry for mercy. "I'll send him running for cover," he said. "Wait and see!"

One day Big Mouth had to go through the woods. As he walked, Big Mouth talked to himself. "If I meet that giant," he said, "I'll wrestle him and win, I will."

"Halt!" cried the giant, appearing suddenly. Big Mouth took one look at who had spoken and jumped into the pile of uprooted trees that the giant had just flung by the side of the path.

"Oh, afraid, are you?" roared the giant.

"Afraid?" cried Big Mouth. "I should say not! I'm — I'm just hunting for the biggest tree to hit you with!"

The giant blinked his eyes. What kind of fellow was this, anyway? He reached in and dragged Big Mouth out into the open by his shirttail. "Let's wrestle!" bellowed the giant.

continued

Poor Big Mouth! Struggling in the giant's grasp, he began to sweat. His eyes bulged, and his teeth chattered with fright. "You — you'd better watch out, you!" he said.

"Watch out?" roared the giant. "Why, look at you — you're so scared, you're covered with sweat! Any minute you'll be begging for mercy!" There was nothing Big Mouth wanted more than mercy. But his tongue just wouldn't say the word.

"I'm — I'm not sweating," he said. "I'm g-g-greasing myself — so you won't be able to hang on to me!" The giant almost lost him at that, for he was slippery. "Well then," snarled the giant, tightening his grip, "why are your eyes bulging? Any minute now you'll beg me to let go so you can breathe again!"

"Oh no, I won't!" squeaked Big Mouth with what little breath he had. "My eyes are bulging because I'm — I'm looking around for a g-g-good p-p-place to throw you!" This was almost too much. With a bellow of rage, the giant held Big Mouth up right in front of his ugly face.

"Well, in that case," he roared, "tell me why your teeth are chattering. Just tell me that!" With such a close view of the giant's teeth, poor Big Mouth nearly fainted. But not even that could stop his bragging tongue. "M-my teeth aren't ch-chattering!" he cried. "I'm — I'm sh-sh-sharpening them to b-bite off your n-n-n-nose!"

And at that, the giant clapped his hand over his nose, dropped Big Mouth to the ground, and ran away deep into the woods. He was never heard from again.

But in case you think this shows that bragging is a good idea, let me tell you the rest. When Big Mouth returned home, nobody believed him — not even his brother.

1. **Who is telling this story?**
   - A Big Mouth
   - B the giant
   - C a narrator

2. **Why did the giant think that Big Mouth would soon be begging for mercy?**
   - A Big Mouth was crying.
   - B Big Mouth began to sweat.
   - C Big Mouth was afraid to open his eyes.

3. **What happened after Big Mouth threatened to bite the giant's nose?**
   - A Big Mouth hid behind a tree.
   - B Big Mouth never bragged again.
   - C The giant dropped Big Mouth to the ground.

4. **Big Mouth said he was greasing himself in order to**
   - A be able to run faster
   - B prevent the giant from holding him
   - C slip past the giant

5. **Why didn't anybody believe Big Mouth's claim that he had fought with the giant?**
   - A Big Mouth always lied to make himself look better.
   - B The giant had already told them the true story.
   - C People believed there was no giant.

6. **When the giant held Big Mouth, the boy's teeth began to *chatter*. What does *chatter* mean?**
   - A turn numb
   - B stiffen from fright
   - C make clicking noises from shaking

7 Fill in the diagram with a word to describe Big Mouth, a word to describe the giant, and a word to describe them both. Use each word only once. Choose from:

1. bragging
2. ferocious
3. foolish
4. trustworthy

[Venn diagram: Big Mouth | BOTH | Giant]

8 The next time Big Mouth tells people a story, listeners will
   ○ A believe him because he never lies
   ○ B ignore him since he is crazy
   ○ C not believe him because he always lies

9 What lesson can be learned from this story?
   ○ A A kindness is never wasted.
   ○ B Equals make the best friends.
   ○ C Those who brag should not expect to be believed.

10 In the story, the giant held Big Mouth up to his face with a "bellow of rage." What does *bellow* mean?
   ○ A loud roar
   ○ B big smile
   ○ C angry look

11 Retell the story in detail.

Directions: Read the selection and answer the questions.

WE'RE ALL IN THE TELEPHONE BOOK
by Langston Hughes (1947)

We're all in the telephone book,
Folks from everywhere on earth —
Anderson to Zabrowski
It's a record of America's worth.

We're all in the telephone book.
There's no priority —
A millionaire like Rockefeller
Is likely to be behind me.

For generations men have dreamed
Of nations united as one.
Just look in your telephone book
To see where that dream's begun.

When Washington crossed the Delaware
And the pillars of tyranny shook,
He started the list of democracy
That's America's telephone book.

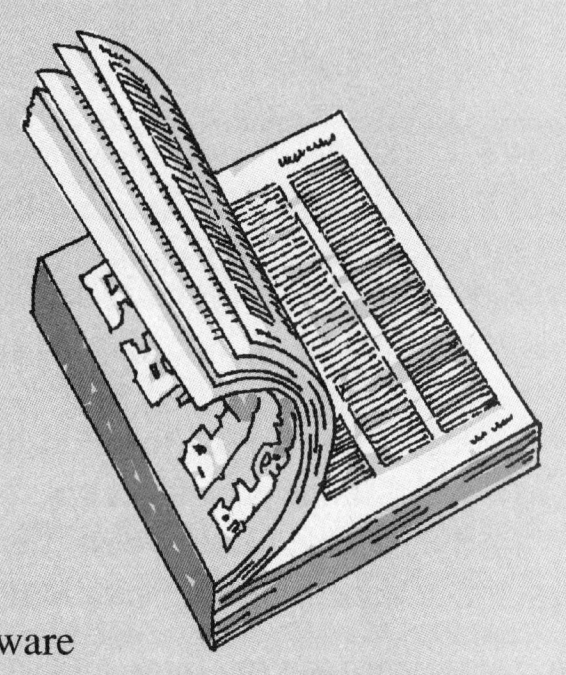

General Washington crossing the Delaware River

12 Which sentence best tells us about this poem?
   - ○ **A** The telephone book symbolizes both the equality and diversity of America.
   - ○ **B** Wealthy people are not usually listed in telephone books.
   - ○ **C** Democracy cannot exist without telecommunications.

13 Which of the following would be the best book to use if you wanted to read more poems by Langston Hughes?
   - ○ **A** *My Life and Times by Langston Hughes*
   - ○ **B** *The Random House Book of Poetry*
   - ○ **C** *The Collected Poems of Langston Hughes*

14 If you were the poet, what would you probably do if someone handed you a telephone book?
   - ○ **A** throw it in the garbage
   - ○ **B** sell it to someone in the Rockefeller family
   - ○ **C** treat it with respect and appreciation

15 The poet says, "There's no priority —" in the sixth line of the poem. What does the word *priority* mean?
   - ○ **A** absence
   - ○ **B** sense of order
   - ○ **C** right or wrong

16 The phrase "It's a record of America's worth," can best be interpreted to mean that it
   - ○ **A** is the best way to determine the wealth of American citizens
   - ○ **B** is not worth much if your name appears in the telephone book
   - ○ **C** shows the true worth of America as a nation of equals

17 When the poet states that Washington "started the list of democracy," he means that
   - ○ **A** the American Revolution introduced the goal of equality
   - ○ **B** Washington invited other nationalities to the United States
   - ○ **C** America has become the world's melting pot

18 **Which pair of lines rhymes?**

○ A For generations men have dreamed
     Of nations united as one

○ B He started the list of democracy
     That's America's telephone book

○ C Folks from everywhere on earth —
     It's a record of America's worth

19 **Which phrase best reflects the poet's feelings about the United States?**

○ A a place where people are too focused on wealth
○ B a country where people of different backgrounds cannot get along
○ C a land in which citizens enjoy equal basic rights

20 **How does the telephone book represent "nations united as one"?**

_____

_____

_____

Directions: Read the selection and answer the questions.

ALVIN AILEY

Alvin Ailey was born in 1931 in Rogers, Texas. As a young boy, he grew up in Navasota, Texas, where he regularly attended church with his mother. His memories of stomping feet, clapping hands, and singing along with the church choir inspired young Alvin to want to study dance.

As a young man, he moved to New York City so he could study under the great dance masters. With a satchel hanging heavy on his shoulder, his shoes rapped a beat on the sidewalk while taxicabs honked their horns. He was glad to be in New York. He took dance classes all over town. At these classes, Alvin met dancers who showed him moves he'd never seen before. So many of the dancers he met were black. Like Alvin, their dreams soared higher than New York's tallest skyscrapers.

In the late 1950s, Alvin gathered some of the dancers he'd seen in classes around the city. He chose the men and women who had just the right moves to dance to his choreography. Alvin told them he wanted to start a modern dance company that would dance to blues and gospel music — the heritage of African American people. Nine dancers believed in Alvin's idea. This was the beginning of the Alvin Ailey American Dance Theatre.

continued

On March 30, 1958, on an old wooden stage at the 92nd Street Y, Alvin and his friends premiered with *Blues Suite,* dances set in a honky-tonk dance hall. Alvin's choreography depicted the blues, that weepy sadness all folks feel now and then. Alvin moved in time to the music, the same way he did when he was a boy. The audience swayed in their seats as Alvin and his company danced. When the show ended, the audience went wild with applause. They stomped and shouted. "More!" they yelled. "More!"

Taking a bow, Alvin let out a breath. He raised his eyes toward heaven, satisfied and proud. Alvin was on his way to making it big. Word spread quickly about him and his dancers. Newspapers hailed him. Under Alvin's leadership, the American Dance Theatre went on to receive international acclaim. Alvin became a famous dancer and choreographer, just as he had always dreamed.

21 The author's main purpose in writing this biography was to
  ○ A describe the birth of dance in New York City
  ○ B show how a determined dancer rose to international fame
  ○ C explain why young people love to dance

22 Which statement is true about Alvin Ailey?
  ○ A He was born in New York City.
  ○ B He learned to dance from his mother.
  ○ C He came to New York City to learn more about dancing.

23 Alvin learned from other dancers in New York how to
- **A** get along with others
- **B** play the piano
- **C** dance in new ways

24 How does the author describe "blues" music?

_____

_____

_____

25 Why was it that the audience "stomped and shouted"?
- **A** They enjoyed Alvin and his dance company.
- **B** They were angry with the conditions of the theatre.
- **C** Many of them were close friends of Alvin Ailey.

26 In the passage, Alvin Ailey is described as a choreographer. A *choreographer* is a person who
- **A** sings songs
- **B** writes music
- **C** creates dance steps

27 The American Dance Theatre went on to receive international acclaim. What does *acclaim* mean?
- **A** popularity
- **B** jobs
- **C** travel

28 Based on what you know about Alvin Ailey from this article, what New York attraction would he most enjoy?
- **A** a trip to the United Nations
- **B** a visit to see a Broadway musical
- **C** a sightseeing ride on the Hudson River

29 Under *Young Boy* put 2 words that help to describe Alvin Ailey while he was growing up. Under *Adult*, put 2 words that describe him as an adult.

AS A YOUNG BOY	AS AN ADULT
_____	_____
_____	_____

30 Summarize the selection.

_____
_____
_____
_____
_____
_____
_____
_____

Directions: Read the selection, then answer the questions.

Dinosaurs

Most of the information we have about dinosaurs comes from our study of fossils. Fossils are the remains of animals and plants that lived long ago. Most of their flesh was eaten by other animals. However, fossils are formed from the hard parts of an animal's body, such as bones, shells or teeth. Eventually, minerals replace the animal parts.

Fossils are often formed when an animal is buried under sand and mud. After a period of time, the soft parts of its body decay, leaving only the bones. Some fossils are large, like a footprint. Other fossils are so tiny that you need a microscope to see them.

Scientists study fossils to help them understand animal life in ancient periods. By studying the rocks and sand in which fossils are found, it is possible for scientists to tell us how certain animals lived long ago.

continued

Scientists believe dinosaurs lived from about 65 million to 225 million years ago. However, people have known about dinosaurs only since the first dinosaur fossils were discovered about 200 years ago. Since then, scientists have used fossil evidence to determine when dinosaurs lived, what they ate, and how large they grew.

No one knows for sure why dinosaurs became extinct, but many theories exist to explain their disappearance. One theory is that an asteroid[1] from space hit the Earth 65 million years ago and blocked out the sunlight. This may have led to dramatic changes in climate and plant life that caused dinosaurs to starve to death. Others theorize that dinosaurs were unable to compete for food with smaller and faster mammals.

(from *The World Almanac for Kids*)

---

[1] large rocks in space that sometimes land on Earth

31 What is the author's main purpose in writing this passage?
- ○ **A** to show the different sizes of fossils
- ○ **B** to outline where fossils can be found
- ○ **C** to describe how fossils help us understand dinosaurs

32 What happens to the soft parts of a dinosaur's body over time?
- ○ **A** They turn to rock.
- ○ **B** They re-grow.
- ○ **C** They decay.

33 What usually happens before a fossil can be formed?
- ○ **A** An animal becomes buried under sand and mud.
- ○ **B** An animal must be eaten by other animals.
- ○ **C** An animal grows very old.

34 How long ago did dinosaurs live on Earth?
- ○ **A** more than 500 million years ago
- ○ **B** between 65 million and 225 million years ago
- ○ **C** less than 65 million years ago

35 The numbered sentences include one *main idea* and two *supporting details*. Use the numbers of the sentences to complete the graphic organizer that follows:

1. Others theorize that dinosaurs were unable to compete for food with smaller and faster mammals.
2. No one knows for sure why dinosaurs became extinct, but many theories exist to explain their disappearance.
3. Some scientists believe a giant asteroid hit the earth, leading to dramatic changes in the climate and plant life that led to dinosaurs starving to death.

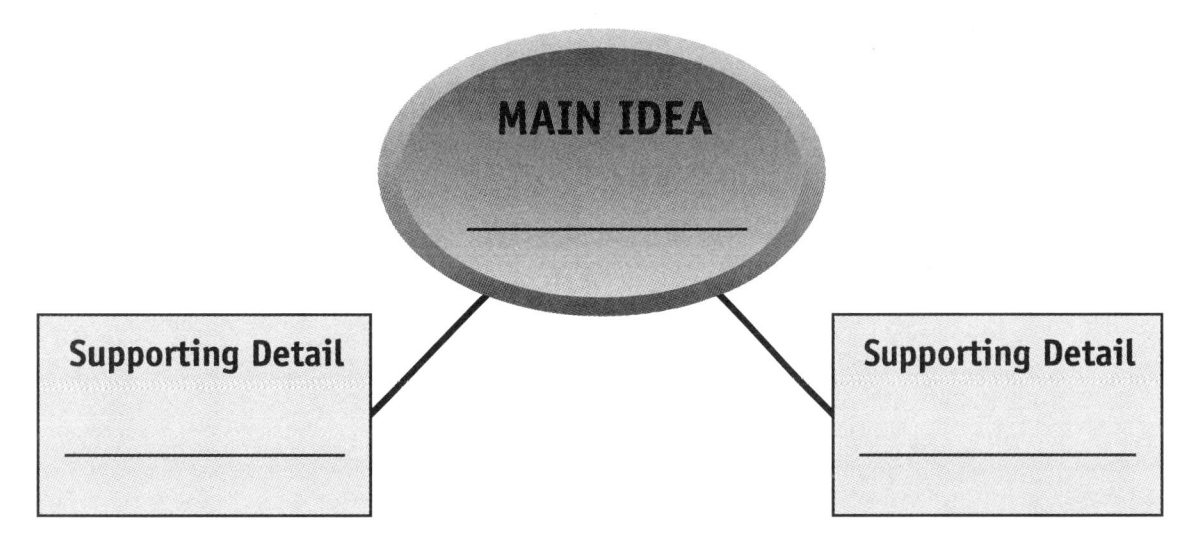

MAIN IDEA
_____

Supporting Detail
_____

Supporting Detail
_____

A Practice Test in Writing

DIRECTIONS FOR THE WRITING SECTION OF THE PRACTICE TEST

Now you are going to take the **Fourth Grade Proficiency Test in Writing.** Please try to do your best work on this test. Remember you are to do your own work — you are not to copy or share your work with anyone.

You will now take the writing section of the test. You are going to do a pre-writing activity and two writing activities, **Exercise A** and **Exercise B.** As you go through the writing test, you will write, then edit, and revise your work with a checklist.

At the bottom of page 177 are the directions for the pre-writing activity. You will silently read these yourself after you start the test.

The pre-writing activity is the first step in the writing process. The pre-writing activity will help you get ideas for both writing activities you will do later. You must think of these ideas on your own. The pre-writing activity will not be scored.

The first writing activity is **Exercise A** — writing a nonfiction article. You will find the directions for **Exercise A** on page 179. You should silently read these to yourself after you start the test. Please note that there is a checklist on the page. The checklist shows what your writing must have to get the best score. Use this checklist when you are writing your story.

Please turn to page 179. You can see that you will do **Exercise A** on this and the following pages. **Exercise A** will be scored.

Next turn to page 182. The second writing activity is **Exercise B** — a friendly letter. The directions for **Exercise B** are on page 174. You will silently read these after you start the test. Please note that there is a checklist on this page. The checklist shows what your writing must have to get the best score. Use the checklist when you are writing your letter.

Please turn to pages 183. You will do **Exercise B** on this page and page 184. **Exercise B** will be scored.

You will use a pencil to write your story and letter. You may make editing changes in your work. If you need to make any changes in your work, make sure you cross out or erase completely the writing you do not want on the test.

You may not use a dictionary or thesaurus in your writing. Spell the words the best way you know. Remember that writers often make changes as they write. Look back at your pre-writing page. You may decide to use some of the ideas that you wrote down.

After 35 minutes your teacher will announce a five-minute break. After you begin, you should continue until the break is announced. If you take the test at home, give yourself a five-minute break halfway through the test. Remember, you will do three writing activities — the pre-writing activity, **Exercise A,** and **Exercise B.** As you finish one activity, go on to the next activity. You may go back to the writing prompt at any time. Now you may begin the test.

EARTH AND WATER AND SKY
by Bryan A. Bushemi

It was a long hike through the woods to the Thinking Pond, but David didn't mind. He liked to spend time there more than he liked doing almost anything else.

When he reached the giant tree along the way, David sat down and took off his backpack. Today David planned to sketch some fallen trees near the Thinking Pond.

David stood up and continued toward the Thinking Pond. Suddenly, he heard a sharp, whining sound like the engine of a high flying jet airplane. It was followed by a *crack!* Like a whip being snapped, only a thousand times louder. Then a ball of fire roared overhead followed by a burning gust of wind.

The shock wave knocked David to the ground, his ears ringing. A second later, he heard an explosive, hissing crash. A rush of air and hot steam rose through the trees, and he covered his head as it washed over him.

He stopped several feet away from the chunk of space rock, which was now giving off a faint sizzling noise. Reaching down, David picked up a small clump of mud oozing around his shoes. He flicked it onto the meteorite's rough surface. The wet dirt hissed and popped, then dried and stuck. The meteorite was definitely too hot to touch.

continued

While he waited for it to cool down, David took his sketch pad out of his backpack. He made a drawing of the rock. He made notes next to the drawing about shading and the faint rainbow tinting of the smoother parts. Even as he was drawing, David could hardly believe he was looking at something that had been flying through space only a few minutes before.

He wondered where the meteorite had come from. Maybe an asteroid or a comet had passed too close to a planet or the Sun, and a chunk of it had been pulled off by gravity. Maybe it had been floating through space for millions of years before Earth's gravitational field caught it and dragged it in.

After several minutes, David looked up. *"What the heck just happened?"* he wondered as he got to his feet. Cautiously but curiously, he headed in the direction of the Thinking Pond. By now David could usually see the shine of sunlight on the water, but today something was different. Covering the last hundred yards quickly, David stopped at the edge of the meadow where the pond lay.

"Whoa!" he said in amazement.

continued

> Before him stretched a dry, cracked-mud crater — all that was left of the Thinking Pond. The water in the fifty-foot diameter pond had evaporated, leaving a huge hole in the forest floor. The baked mud rippled out from the center in wide, shallow waves. In the middle of the crater, half-buried in the ground, was a rounded, melted lump of something that looked like rock. It was a little larger than a baseball.
>
> "I can't believe it!" David whispered, awe-struck. "It's a meteorite."

Now you will do some thinking and planning for a story of your own. You will make up and write a story, and then you will write a letter about it.

PRE-WRITING

Directions: What might happen if a large meteorite were to strike your neighborhood. How would such an event affect your neighborhood? Who would be most affected by such an event? Take time to read and answer the questions that follow. The pre-writing activity will help you get ideas for the story you will make up. The pre-writing work will not be scored.

1. **What might happen if a large meteorite were to strike your neighborhood?** Write as many details as you can think of about such an event. Then put a check next to the events you want to use in your essay.

2. **How would such an event affect your neighborhood?** Think about how a large meteorite hitting your community would bring about changes. Write as many details as you can think of. Then put a check by the ones that you choose for your essay.

3. **Who might be most affected by such an event?** Who would be hurt? Who would escape? Write down how as many people in your neighborhood as you can think of would be affected. Then put a check next to the people you want to include in your essay.

Exercise A:

A FICTIONAL NARRATIVE — A Story You Make Up

Now you are going to do two writing activities. First, you are going to make up or invent a story about what might happen to your neighborhood if it were struck by a large meteorite, and then you will write a letter to a pen pal about one act of heroism that occurred during the chaos when the meteorite struck your neighborhood.

The story you write on the following pages will be scored. Look at the box below. It shows what your best paper must have.

☑ CHECKLIST

I will earn my best score if:
- ☐ My made-up story tells what happened.
- ☐ My made-up story tells about the impact of such an event.
- ☐ My made-up story tells who would affected by such an event.
- ☐ My made-up story has a beginning, middle, and end.
- ☐ I use words that make my meaning clear. I do not use the same words over and over.
- ☐ I try to spell the words correctly.
- ☐ My sentences and proper names begin with a capital letter.
- ☐ My sentences end with a period, an exclamation mark, or a question mark.

Directions: You will make up a story about the effects of a meteorite hitting your neighborhood. Your story will tell how it came about, and who was affected. Look back at the pre-writing page in which you answered certain questions, and use the things you checked for your made-up story. Your story should make sense and have a beginning, a middle, and an end. Be sure to use words that make your meaning clear. Write your fictional narrative on the following pages.

Exercise A: Fictional Narrative — A Story You Make Up

Name: _____ Teacher: _____

When you finish writing your story, use the checklist to revise and edit your work. When you have finished checking your story and you are satisfied with it, you may go ahead to the second activity, **Exercise B.**

Exercise B:
A FRIENDLY LETTER

The letter you write will be scored. Look at the box below. The box shows what your letter must have to get your best score.

✔ CHECKLIST

I will earn my best score if:
- ❏ My letter tells about someone who acted heroically.
- ❏ My letter gives details about what they did.
- ❏ My letter tells why I think that act was heroic.
- ❏ My letter is complete.
- ❏ I use the form of a letter with a greeting, a body, and a closing.
- ❏ I use words that make my meaning clear in my letter.
- ❏ I try to spell the words correctly.
- ❏ My sentences and proper names begin with a capital letter.
- ❏ My sentences end with a period, an exclamation mark, or a question mark.

Directions: Write a letter to a friend telling him or her about someone in your neighborhood who acted heroically after the meteorite struck your community. Look back at your pre-writing page for ideas. You may decide to use one of the ideas that you wrote down *but did not use in your story*. Write your letter on the following pages.

Name: _____   **Teacher:** _____

Dear _____ ,

When you finish writing your friendly letter, use the checklist to revise and edit your work. If you take this practice test in class, take out a book to read or other work to do at your desk when you have finished checking your work and you are satisfied with it. Or you may go back to your first writing and work on it some more.

APPENDICES

A HANDBOOK OF GRAMMAR AND WRITING MECHANICS AND GUIDE TO THE INTERPRETATION OF DATA

The materials in these appendices provide a reference you can consult at any time in the course of your review. The *Handbook of Grammar and Writing Mechanics* summarizes some of the basic rules fourth grade students are expected to apply in their writing. Following the *Handbook* is a separate guide to the interpretation of data in graphic or visual form. This section will help you review for different tables, maps or graphs that could appear on the **Fourth Grade Proficiency Tests in Reading and Writing.**

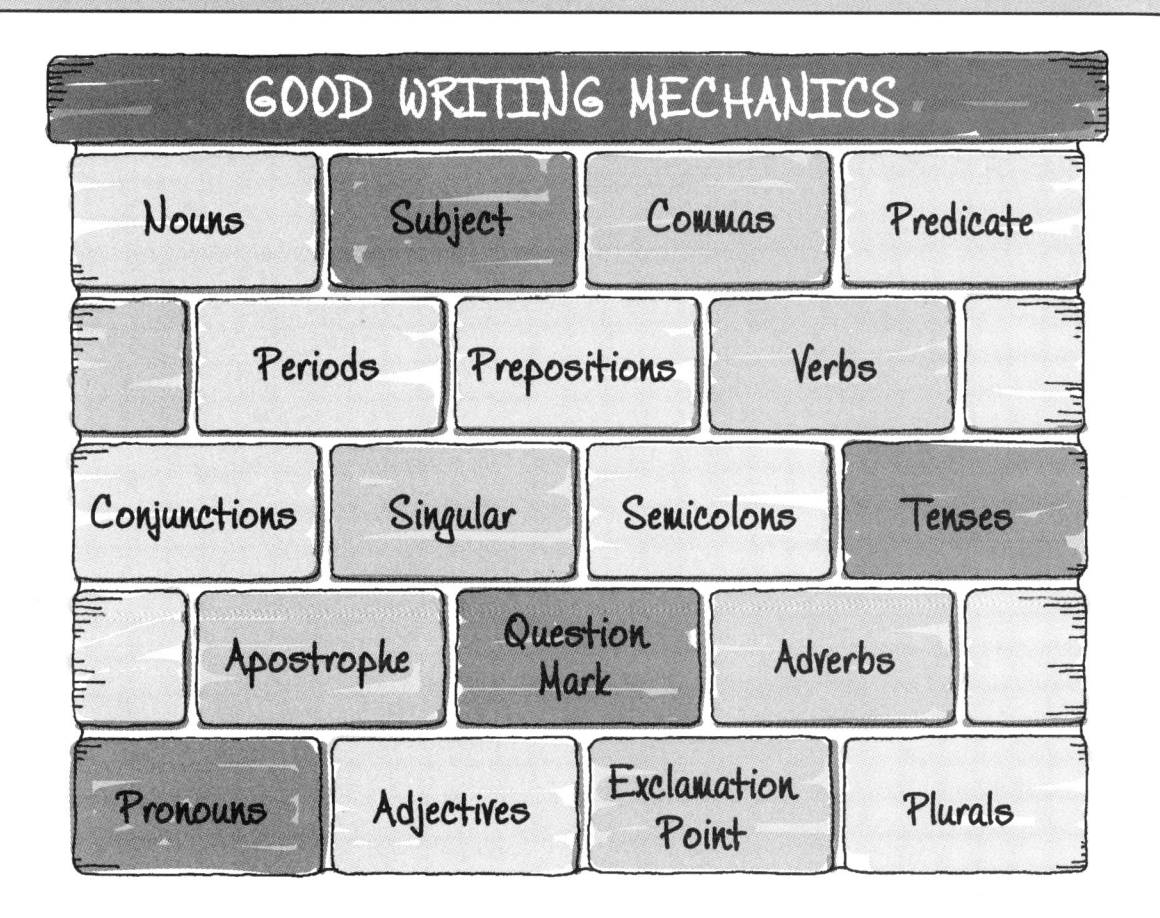

GOOD WRITING MECHANICS

- Nouns
- Subject
- Commas
- Predicate
- Periods
- Prepositions
- Verbs
- Conjunctions
- Singular
- Semicolons
- Tenses
- Apostrophe
- Question Mark
- Adverbs
- Pronouns
- Adjectives
- Exclamation Point
- Plurals

A HANDBOOK OF GRAMMAR AND WRITING MECHANICS

The **Fourth Grade Proficiency Test in Writing** requires you to follow the conventions of standard written English. This handbook will review each of these elements of good writing.

THE "EQUIPMENT"

Writing is like playing a game. The object of the game is to communicate to the reader the thoughts you want the reader to know. In order to play this game, you must first be familiar with the equipment you will use. The basic pieces in the game of writing are words. It is how you put these words together that allows you to communicate your meaning. The basic unit of organizing words is called a *sentence*.

THE SENTENCE

Every sentence in the English language expresses a complete idea. Each sentence has a *subject* and a *predicate*. The **subject** is who or what the sentence is about. It may be one or several words. The **predicate** is what the subject does or what happens to the subject in the sentence. It provides the action of the sentence. Like the subject, the predicate may have one or more words. Together, they make a complete thought.

Subject	Predicate
The crocodile	ate the clock.
The girl	walked the plank.
Captain Hook	baked the cake.

Do not be fooled by a group of words that look like a sentence. If the words do not express a complete thought, they do not make a sentence. The examples on the following page are ***not*** sentences:

| After I went shopping. | Until we sign the paper. |
| Because I like you. | The car is going to. |

> **SOME RULES FOR SENTENCES**
>
> ★ The *first word* of a sentence always starts with a *capital* letter.
> ★ Sentence endings depend on the content of the sentence:
>   • Sentences that make a statement end with a **period** (.).
>   • Sentences that ask a question end with a **question mark** (?).
>   • Sentences that show strong feelings, such as surprise, laughter, or a strong emotion end in an **exclamation point** (!).

PARTS OF SPEECH

The words that make up sentences are called **parts of speech.** The major parts of speech are:

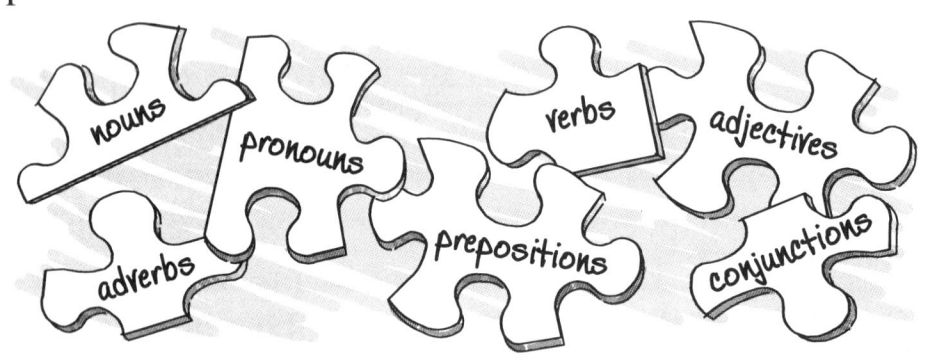

nouns, pronouns, verbs, adjectives, adverbs, prepositions, conjunctions

NOUNS

The subject of a sentence is always a *noun* or *pronoun*. A **noun** is a word that names a person, place, or thing. Nouns can appear in both the subject and the predicate of a sentence.

Subject	Predicate
The *car*	went up the *hill.*
Christopher	loved to eat *donuts.*

SOME RULES FOR NOUNS

★ A proper noun that names a particular person, place or thing starts with a capital letter: *Detroit, Maple Street, United Nations*.

★ Most nouns become plural by adding *s*. To form the plural of nouns ending in *s, z, x, ch,* or *sh,* add *es*. Nouns ending in a consonant and *y* usually eliminate the *y* and add *ies*. A few nouns do not change in plural.

Singular	Plural	Singular	Plural
hat	hats	story	stories
church	churches	sheep	sheep

★ Nouns usually form possessives by adding an apostrophe (') and *s*. A plural noun usually shows possession by adding the apostrophe after the *s*.

Singular Noun	Plural Noun
These are *Jack's* books.	These are the *teams'* schedules.

PRONOUNS

It would be boring if we kept repeating the same noun over and over again when we spoke or wrote. A **pronoun** is a word that takes the place of a noun used earlier in a speech or writing. The most common pronouns are ***I, we, you, he, she, it,*** and ***they***. These pronouns are used in place of the subject of the sentence. When a pronoun is used, it must be clear what noun (or *antecedent*) the pronoun is replacing.

The *circus wagon* went up the hill.
It was driven by Bozo the clown.

Bozo loved to jump off the trapeze.
He also liked wiggling his ears.

Sometimes the pronoun is the object of the action of the sentence. Common **object pronouns** are: ***me, us, you, him, her, it,*** and ***them***.

Christopher loved to cut *coconuts*. He ate *them* almost everyday.

Pronouns can also show ownership or possession. The most important **possessive pronouns** are: *my, your, his, her, its, our* and *their*.

> *Jason* stood on *his* nose. *His* mother watched from *her* window.

Some pronouns can also be used to indicate questions about a group of nouns. They clarify which part of a group of things is being referred to. **Which, who** and **what** are important pronouns that ask questions.

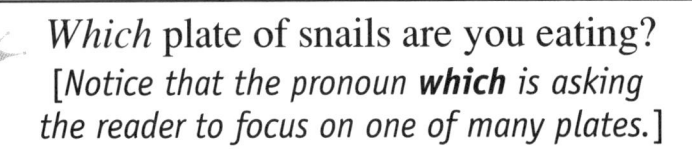

> *Which* plate of snails are you eating?
> [Notice that the pronoun **which** is asking the reader to focus on one of many plates.]

> *Who* was the first person to eat cheese on the moon?
> [Notice how the pronoun **who** is narrowing the group of many possible people down to one.]

SOME RULES FOR PRONOUNS

★ It should be clear to the reader what noun the pronoun is replacing. The pronoun should be the same gender (*male* or *female*) and number (*singular* or *plural*) as the noun.

★ ***It's*** is a contraction for ***it is.*** ***Its*** without an apostrophe shows possession.
- *It's* time to go home.
- The thief took the bicycle from *its* owner.

★ Word Choice: confusion between **there — their — they're**
- *There* means a place. The monster is over *there*.
- *Their* shows possession. *Their* taxi is waiting.
- *They're* is a contraction for *they are*. *They're* ready to leave.

★ Word Choice: confusion between **your** and **you're**
- *Your* shows ownership. Is this *your* elephant?
- *You're* is a contraction for *you are*. Susan, *you're* very kind.

VERBS

Sentences would have little meaning if they just had nouns and pronouns. **Verbs** are words that tell us what a person or thing is doing. For example, action verbs such as *walk, jump* and *run* tell us what the subject of a sentence does or feels. Strong action words create clear mental images for the reader.

The laughing cow *jumped* over the fence.
The spoon *danced* with the fork.

Some special verbs tell the reader about the characteristics of the subject. These are referred to as linking verbs. The most common is the verb **be** in its various forms.

A ball *is* round.
José *was* twenty years old.

Verbs also tell us *when* an action happens. They take different forms, known as **tenses,** to express the past, present or future.

★ **Present Tense.** To make the present tense of most verbs, add *s* if the subject is singular. You can usually use the plain form of the verb for plural subjects, *I* and *you*.

Captain Kirk *likes* school.
The Klingons *like* to play basketball.
I *like* strawberries.

★ **Past Tense.** To make the past tense of most verbs, add *ed*.

Spock *enjoyed* school.
Dinosaurs once *roamed* in this area.

★ **Future Tense.** To make the future tense of most verbs, use *will* or *is going to* in front of the plain form of the verb.

| José *will* attend high school next year. |
| Joan *is going to* play the piano for her aunt. |

The verb *be* is a special verb. It is often used as a helping verb with action verbs. It takes special forms.

	Present	Past	Future	
I	am	was	will *be*	playing ball.
You	are	were	will *be*	playing ball.
He, she, it	is	was	will *be*	playing ball.
They	are	were	will *be*	playing ball.

SOME RULES FOR VERBS

★ Be sure to use the plural form of the verb with plural subjects, and the singular form with singular subjects. This is known as subject-verb agreement. Most action verbs add *s* with singular subjects and take the plain form of the verb with plural subjects.

- *John plays* baseball.
- *John and Susan play* baseball

★ Many common verbs take an irregular form in the past tense:

Present Tense
- give
- get

Past Tense
- gave
- got

EXPANDING THE SENTENCE

The most common pattern for organizing nouns, pronouns, and verbs is *subject-verb-object*. But a sentence with just nouns, pronouns, and verbs would give only a very basic idea to the reader. Such a sentence is like a skeleton without flesh. A world with only nouns and verbs lacks color.

As a writer, you will want to describe some things in greater detail. You will want to say what your subject is like. You will want to describe *how* something is done. To do these things, you will have to make use of other parts of speech. *Adjectives, adverbs, prepositions* and *conjunctions* help make your sentences more descriptive. They give your reader a greater understanding of the images and ideas you want to communicate.

ADJECTIVES

Words that describe nouns are called **adjectives.** They tell us what the noun is like, and usually go before the noun. Adjectives add mood and color to a sentence. Think about all five senses when considering adjectives to describe a noun. What does the thing look like, sound like, smell like, or even feel like?

> The *green* car went up the *large* hill.
> [*Notice how the adjectives give color and size to the nouns in the sentence.*]
>
> A *wiggling* bug crawled across the *dark* room.

Adjectives can also be used to compare people, places or things. To compare one thing to another, add *er* to the adjective. To say one thing is the most or best out of more than two, add *est.*

> Jack is tall*er* than Eric.
>
> Abdul is the tall*est* boy in the class.

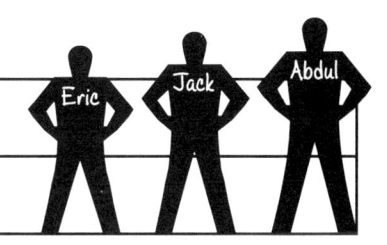

The special adjectives *a, an,* and *the* are known as **articles.**

SOME RULES FOR ADJECTIVES

★ Most action verbs can be turned into adjectives by adding *ing:* laugh*ing,* runn*ing,* smil*ing.*

★ *A* is used before a consonant. *An* is used before words beginning with a vowel:
- *a car, a book, a church, a store*
- *an iceberg, an egg, an apple, an uncle*

★ Some adjectives take irregular forms for comparing:
- good   better   best
- —   more   most
- bad   worse   worst

ADVERBS

Just as adjectives tell us more about nouns, words known as **adverbs** tell us more about verbs, adjectives or other adverbs. Adverbs give greater clarity to the action of a sentence. They tell us where, when or how an action happens.

> The space ship flew *quickly* over our heads.
>
> Brian *often* goes to the same planet as his mother.

SOME RULES FOR ADVERBS

★ Many adjectives can be changed into adverbs by adding *ly*
- quick → quick*ly*
- slow → slow*ly*

★ Not all adverbs end in *ly.* Other common adverbs include: *often, very, sometimes,* and *never*

★ *Good* is not an adverb. It is an adjective. Use *well* as the adverb.
- Correct: He played *well.*
- Incorrect: He played *good.*

PREPOSITIONS

In writing, we sometimes need to describe nouns and verbs with a whole phrase — a group of words that is not a sentence. A **prepositional phrase** is a group of words beginning with a *preposition* and ending with a noun or pronoun. The preposition connects the noun or pronoun to another part of the sentence by describing their relationship. Some of the most common prepositions are *at, on, about, with, over, under, between, after, before, of* and *to*. There are many ways to relate a prepositional phrase to the rest of a sentence. Two of the most important are time and place.

At seven o'clock the green car drove quickly up the large hill.
[*Notice how the prepositional phrase connects the action of this sentence to a period of time.*]

The alligator ate bread and butter *after school.*

SOME RULES FOR PREPOSITIONS

★ If the object of the preposition is a pronoun, it must be an *object pronoun*. For example: "The elephant gave an egg to me." (*not I*)

★ Do not use a comma after a prepositional phrase.

CONJUNCTIONS

Another way to expand the basic sentence is to bring two subjects, verbs or sentences together. **Conjunctions** are parts of speech that allow us to bring words, phrases, or sentences together. The conjunctions **and, or** and **but** are commonly used to join two separate sentences together.

Sam went to the store, *and* Ashley went to the movies.

Captain Kirk is smart, *but* Mr. Spock is smarter.

Some other conjunctions are *as, although, because, since* and *when.* These special conjunctions allow us to add a separate *clause* with its own subject and predicate to an existing sentence.

> *Although it was in a time-warp,* the spaceship flew straight ahead.
>
> Justin went to the store *because his mother needed sugar.*

Notice how these separate clauses actually tell us something about the noun or verb of the existing sentence. They often describe a **condition** or explain *why* the action in the existing sentence took place.

A RULE FOR CONJUNCTIONS

★ Clauses introduced by conjunctions such as *although, because, since, as* and *when* are never complete sentences by themselves.

In writing, it can help to start your sentences with a basic framework of nouns and verbs. Then enrich your sentence by saying more about the subject and the action. Use adjectives, adverbs, prepositional phrases and clauses to describe the subject and tell more about the action of the sentence.

OTHER RULES OF THE GAME

Now that you are familiar with the basic equipment used in the game of writing, let's look at some of the more advanced rules that you will need to play the "game."

SPELLING

In order to be understood, you must use words that your reader is able to recognize. There is common agreement about the spelling of words. You must follow these conventions for others to understand you. The following are some of the most important rules for spelling that fifth graders are expected to know:

RULE 1: Changing a final *y* to an *i*.

When a noun ends in *y* after a consonant, change it to an *i* and add *es* to make it plural.

story	stories
city	cities

RULE 2: Dropping the final *e*.

When a noun ends in a consonant plus an *e*, drop the final *e* before adding *ing*.

hide	hiding
love	loving

RULE 3: Words with *ei* and *ie*.

In general, use the following well-known rhyme for spelling words with *ei* and *ie:* "Use *i* before *e*, except after *c*, or when sounding like *ay*, as in neighbor or weigh." Here is how some common words follow the rule:

p*ie*ce	ch*ie*f	c*ei*ling	sl*ei*gh

However, there are some exceptions to the rule, such as:

w*ei*rd	s*ei*ze

RULE 4: Plural of nouns ending with *f*.

If a noun ends in *f*, change the *f* to *v* and then add *es* to make it plural.

wolf	wolves
shelf	shelves

RULE 5: Words ending in *ght*.

Some words end with *ght* to make the sound *t*. Do not be confused by their spelling.

eight	night	thought

RULE 6: Practice, practice, practice.

You should practice spelling any words you occasionally misspell. Because English has been influenced by many other languages, the same sound is not always spelled the same way:

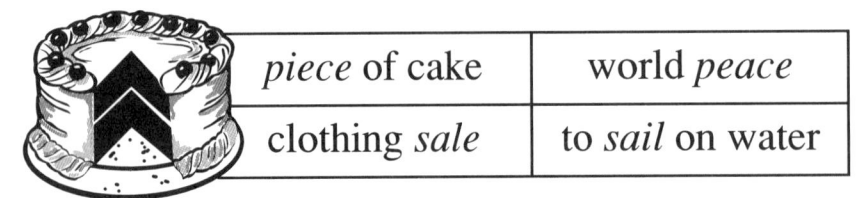

piece of cake	world *peace*
clothing *sale*	to *sail* on water

CAPITALIZATION AND PUNCTUATION

In addition to correct spelling, good writing requires proper capitalization and punctuation. Capitalization and punctuation are like street signs. They tell the reader when to go, stop or pause. They also help the reader to see how the writer's ideas are connected.

CAPITALIZATION

In dealing with capitalization, you should keep the following rules in mind:

★ *Days, months, holidays, book titles, streets, cities* and *countries* begin with capital letters.

★ Proper nouns, such as *people's names,* begin with capital letters.

★ Always begin a sentence with a capital letter and always capitalize the pronoun *I.*

COMMAS

Commas are used in sentences to show the reader where to pause. In dealing with commas, you should keep the following rules in mind:

★ Use commas to separate the day of the month from the year in a date, and to separate the date from the rest of the sentence.

> On July 20, 1969, the United States landed a man on the moon.

★ Use commas to separate the name of a city or place from the state in which it is located.

> Lake Oswego, Oregon   Springfield, Illinois

★ Use commas between words in a series.

> He ate ice cream, cake and candy.

★ Use commas to set off phrases.

> Mr. Jones, a quiet man, was very excited.

★ Use commas before the conjunctions *and, or* and *but* in compound sentences.

> Jack went up the hill, and Jill fetched a pail of water.

OTHER PUNCTUATION

★ Use commas and quotation marks to indicate direct speech. If the sentence ends with the quotation, put quotation marks outside the closing punctuation of the sentence.

> Jack said, "Jill went to fetch a pail of water."

★ Apostrophes are used to show possession or in contractions to indicate that letters are missing.

> It was Robert's book.   He can't do it.

NOTES

INTERPRETING DIFFERENT TYPES OF DATA

One or more of the reading passages on the **Fourth Grade Proficiency Test in Reading** may have information, known as **data,** presented in graphic or visual form.

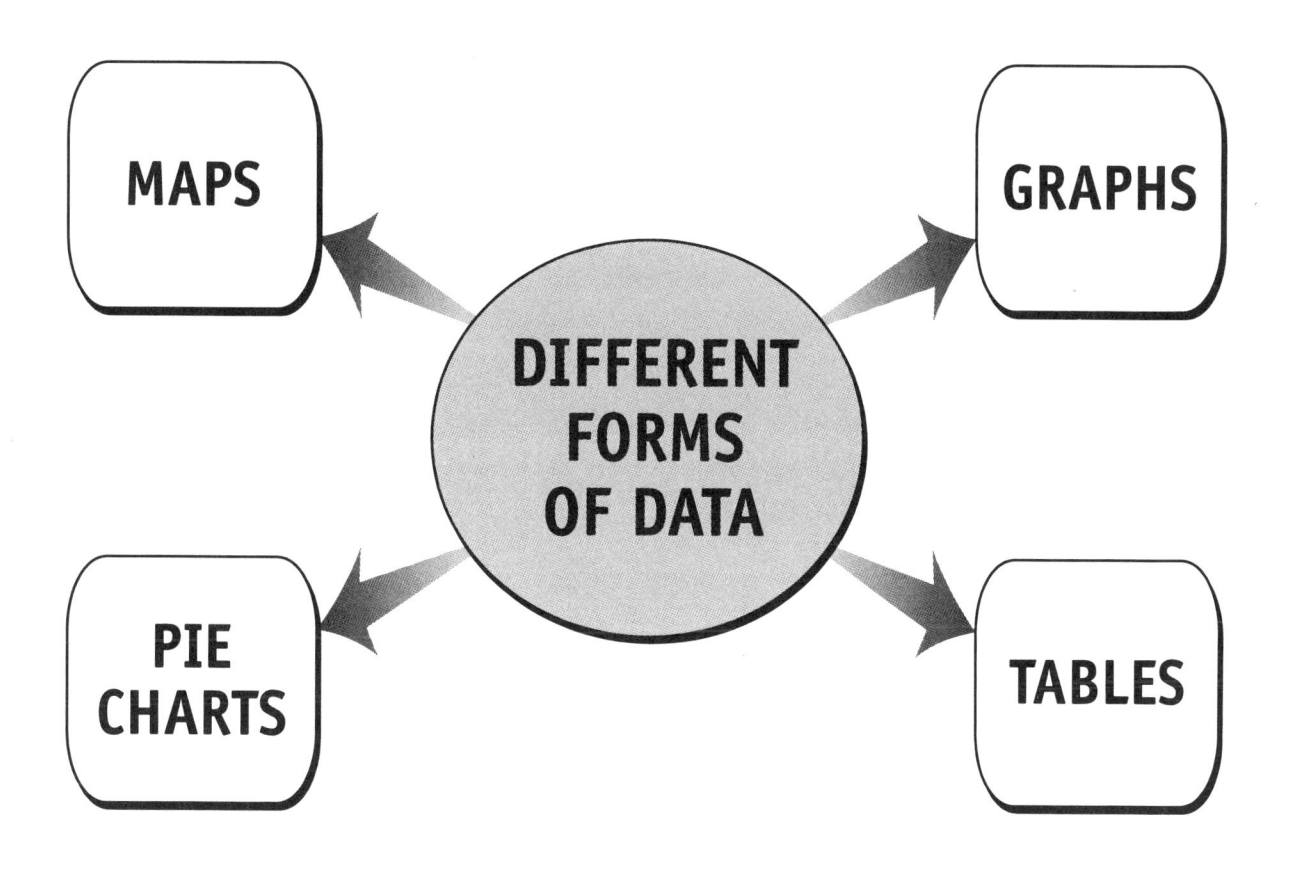

DIFFERENT FORMS OF DATA
- MAPS
- GRAPHS
- PIE CHARTS
- TABLES

This appendix will guide you through each of the major forms of data that might appear on the test.

MAPS

A **map** is a drawing that represents a geographical area. There is almost no limit to the kind of information that can be shown on a map.

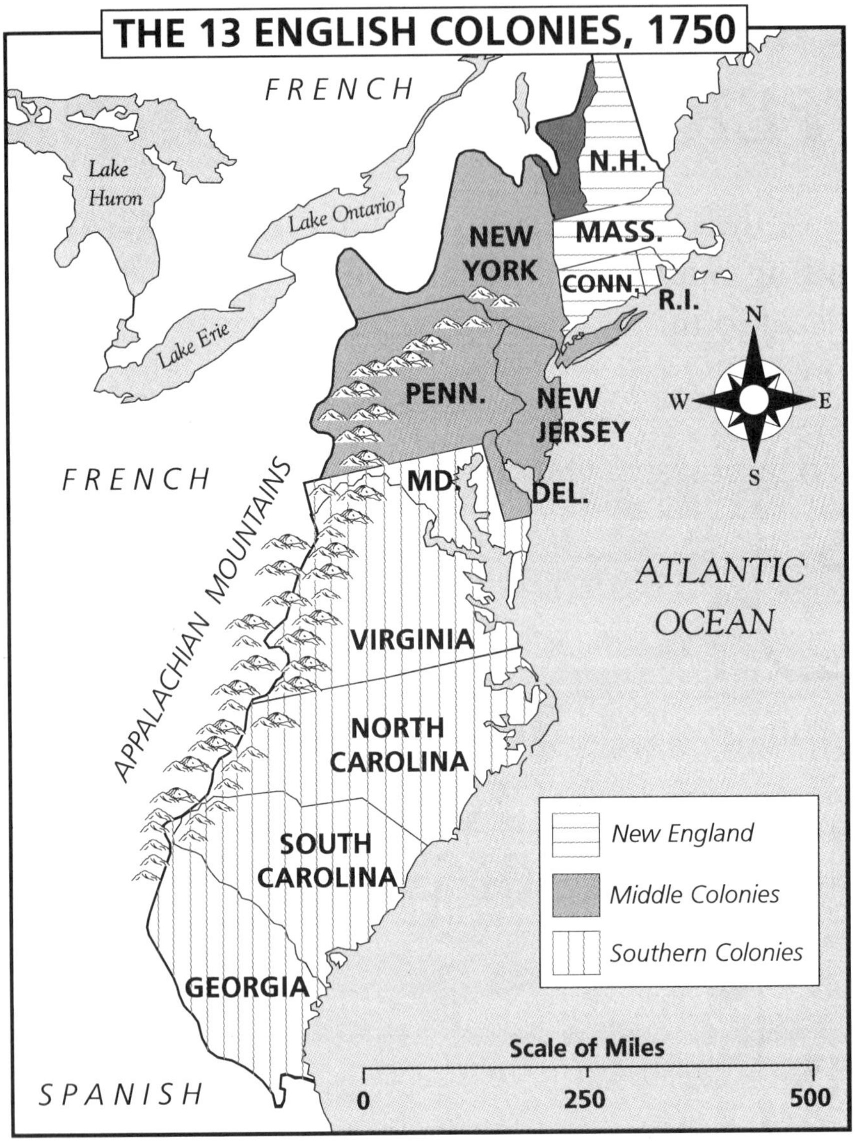
THE 13 ENGLISH COLONIES, 1750
FRENCH
Lake Huron
Lake Ontario
Lake Erie
N.H.
NEW YORK
MASS.
CONN.
R.I.
PENN.
NEW JERSEY
MD.
DEL.
FRENCH
APPALACHIAN MOUNTAINS
VIRGINIA
NORTH CAROLINA
SOUTH CAROLINA
GEORGIA
SPANISH
ATLANTIC OCEAN
N
W
E
S
New England
Middle Colonies
Southern Colonies
Scale of Miles
0
250
500

KEYS TO UNDERSTANDING A MAP

★ **Read the Title.** The title of the map tells you what kind of information is presented. For example, the title of the map above is: *The 13 English Colonies, 1750*. This map shows the location of the English colonies in North America in the year 1750.

INTERPRETING DIFFERENT TYPES OF DATA   203

★ **Look at the Legend.** The legend unlocks the information on the map. It identifies what each symbol represents. For example, in this map:

- **horizontal lines** ▤ show the location of the New England Colonies.

- **light gray areas** ▢ show the location of the Middle Colonies.

- **vertical lines** ▥ show the location of the Southern Colonies.

CHECKING YOUR UNDERSTANDING

Name **two** English colonies located in New England:

1. _____

2. _____

Name **one** English colony located in the South:

1. _____

GRAPHS

Graphs generally use bars or lines to represent amounts.

A **bar graph** is a chart made up of parallel bars with different lengths. A bar graph is often used to make a comparison of two or more things.

IMMIGRANTS TO THE U. S. BY REGION, 1900 - 1995

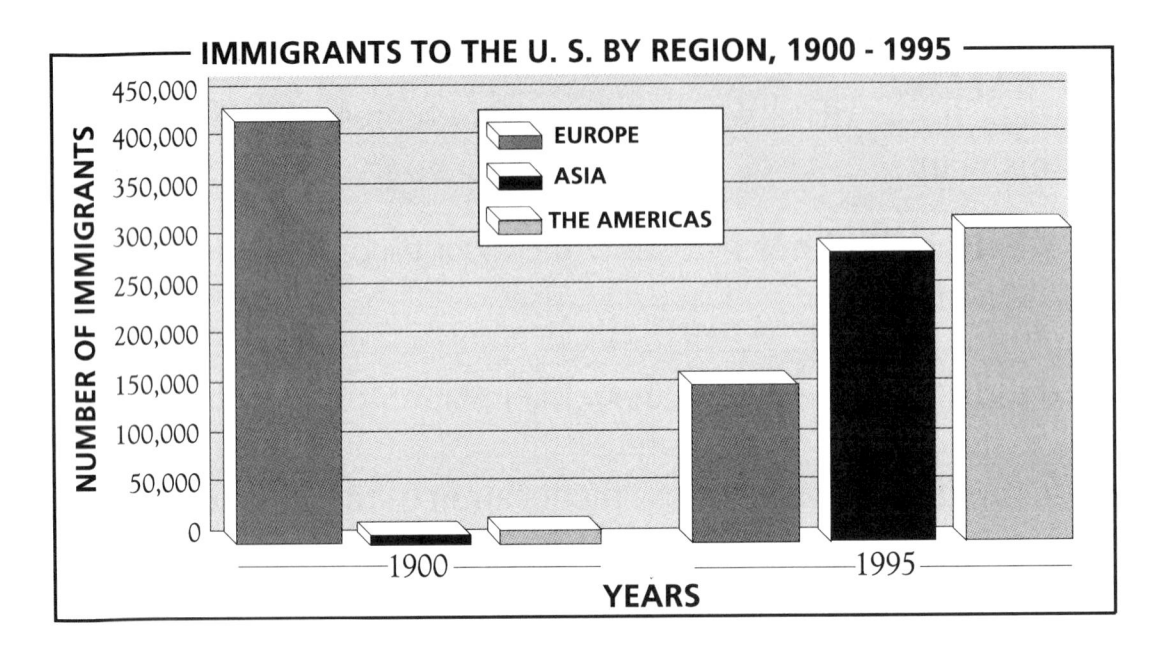

KEYS TO UNDERSTANDING A BAR GRAPH

★ **Read the Title.** The title tells you the topic of the graph.

★ **Look at the Legend.** The legend shows what each bar represents. For example, the

- **dark gray bars** represent *Europe*

- **black bars** represent *Asia*

- **light gray bars** represent the *Americas* (*North, Central, and South America*)

★ **Examine the Bars.** The length of each bar represents a specific amount. The number on the line at the left of the graph gives the number that a particular bar represents.

CHECKING YOUR UNDERSTANDING

According to the bar graph above, about how many immigrants came to the United States from Asia in 1995? _____

A **line graph** is a chart composed of a series of points connected by a line. A line graph is often used to show how something has changed over a period of time.

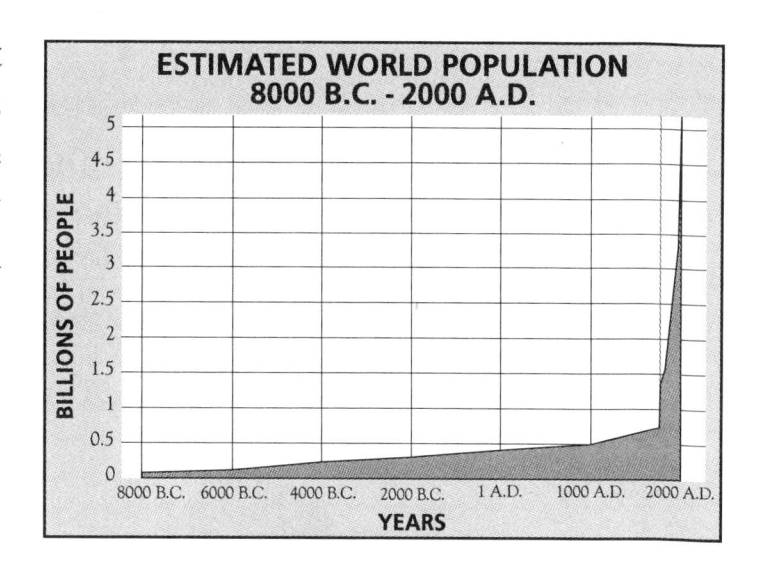

ESTIMATED WORLD POPULATION 8000 B.C. – 2000 A.D.

KEYS TO UNDERSTANDING A LINE GRAPH

★ **Read the Title.** The title tells you the topic of the graph.

★ **Look at the Legend.** A legend tells you what each line represents. Sometimes there is no need for a separate legend, such as in the line graph above. Here there is only one line.

★ **Examine the Axis.** Each line graph has a vertical and a horizontal axis.

- The **vertical axis** runs from bottom to top and measures the size of what is shown in the graph. In the graph above, the vertical axis measures the number of people in the world.

- The **horizontal axis** runs from left to right and measures the passage of time. In this graph, it identifies the dates for which the population of the world is given.

CHECKING YOUR UNDERSTANDING

On the line graph above, what was the population of the world in 1000 A.D.? _____

PIE CHARTS

A **pie chart,** also called a **circle graph,** is a circle divided into sections of different sizes. Each slice is a fraction of the whole pie. If you add up all the slices they will equal 100%. Pie charts are often used to show the relationship between a whole and its parts.

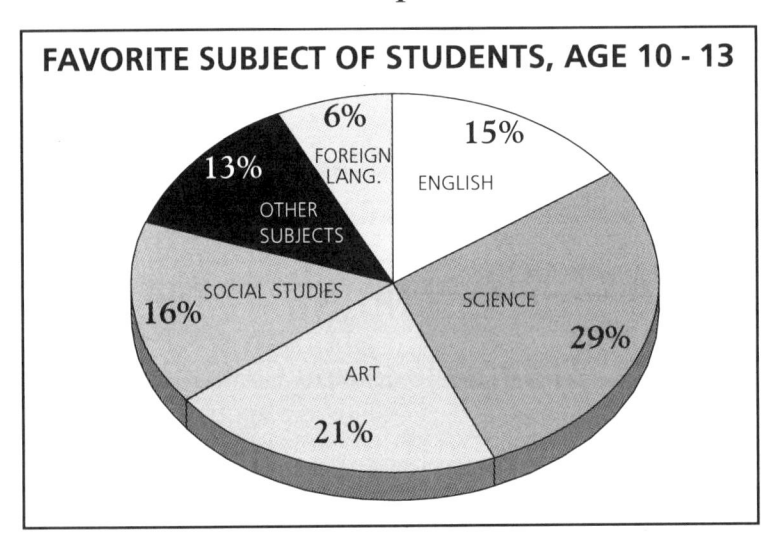

FAVORITE SUBJECT OF STUDENTS, AGE 10 - 13

- Foreign Lang. 6%
- English 15%
- Science 29%
- Art 21%
- Social Studies 16%
- Other Subjects 13%

KEYS TO UNDERSTANDING A PIE CHART

★ **Read the Title.** The title tells you the overall topic.

★ **Examine the Legend.** Sometimes a pie chart has a legend showing what each slice of the pie represents. If the information is shown on the slices, as on this pie chart, a legend is not needed.

★ **Look at the Slices of the Pie.** In this pie, each slice represents the favorite subject of some students. For example, 29% of students age 10 to 13 chose science as their favorite subject.

CHECKING YOUR UNDERSTANDING

Which subject was least popular among students age 10 to 13?

_____

TABLES

A **table** is an arrangement of words or numbers in columns. A table is often used to organize large amounts of information so that facts can be easily located and compared.

CHARITABLE GIVING IN THE UNITED STATES, 1991–1995

Year	Individuals	Businesses
1991	$96.10 billion	$5.62 billion
1992	$98.38 billion	$5.92 billion
1993	$102.13 billion	$6.26 billion
1994	$104.53 billion	$6.88 billion
1995	$116.23 billion	$7.40 billion

KEYS TO UNDERSTANDING A TABLE

★ **Read the Title.** The title of the table tells you its overall topic.

★ **Look at the Categories.** Each table is made up of various categories of information. These categories are named in the column headings across the top of the table.

★ **Finding Information.** To find specific information, you must find where the columns and rows of information intersect or cross.

CHECKING YOUR UNDERSTANDING

Identify the categories used in this table: _____

Identify the year in which individuals contributed the most money to charity and the amount they gave.

Year: _____   Amount: _____